HISTORY OF THE CAMP-MEETING AND GROUNDS AT WESLEYAN GROVE, MARTHA'S VINEYARD,

For Eleven Years Ending with the Meeting of 1869

B. L. Fisher Library Camp Meeting Series ; vol. 5.
Series editor: Robert A. Danielson, Ph.D.

HISTORY OF THE CAMP-MEETING AND GROUNDS AT WESLEYAN GROVE, MARTHA'S VINEYARD,

For Eleven Years Ending with the Meeting of 1869

BY
REV. H. VINCENT

First Fruits Press
Wilmore, Kentucky
c2016

History of the camp-meeting and grounds at Wesleyan Grove, Martha's Vineyard for the eleven years ending with the meeting of 1869, with glances at the earlier years.
By Rev. H. Vincent.

First Fruits Press, ©2016
Previously published by Lee and Shepard, 1870.

ISBN: 9781621716600 (print), 9781621716617 (digital), 9781621716624 (kindle)

Digital version at http://place.asburyseminary.edu/firstfruitsheritagematerial/138/

First Fruits Press is a digital imprint of the Asbury Theological Seminary, B.L. Fisher Library. Asbury Theological Seminary is the legal owner of the material previously published by the Pentecostal Publishing Co. and reserves the right to release new editions of this material as well as new material produced by Asbury Theological Seminary. Its publications are available for noncommercial and educational uses, such as research, teaching and private study. First Fruits Press has licensed the digital version of this work under the Creative Commons Attribution Noncommercial 3.0 United States License. To view a copy of this license, visit http://creativecommons.org/licenses/by-nc/3.0/us/.

For all other uses, contact:

First Fruits Press
B.L. Fisher Library
Asbury Theological Seminary
204 N. Lexington Ave.
Wilmore, KY 40390
http://place.asburyseminary.edu/firstfruits

Vincent, H. (Hebron), 1805-1890.
History of the camp-meeting and grounds at Wesleyan Grove, Martha's Vineyard for the eleven years ending with the meeting of 1869, with glances at the earlier years / by H. Vincent. – Wilmore, Kentucky: First Fruits Press, ©2016.
   258 pages; 23 cm.--(B.L. Fisher Library camp meeting series; volume 2)
   Reprint. Previously published: Boston: Lee and Shepard, 1870.
   ISBN - 13: 9781621716600 (paperback)
   1. Methodist Episcopal Church--Massachusetts--History. 2. Camp meetings--Massachusetts--Martha's Vineyard--History. 3. Martha's Vineyard (Mass.)--Church history. I. Title. II. Asbury Theological Seminary. B.L. Fisher Library. Camp meeting series; volume 2.
BX8476.M3 V73 2016

Cover design by Jonathan Ramsay

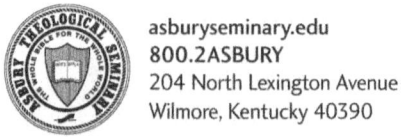

First Fruits Press
The Academic Open Press of Asbury Theological Seminary
204 N. Lexington Ave., Wilmore, KY 40390
859-858-2236
first.fruits@asburyseminary.edu
asbury.to/firstfruits

HISTORY

OF THE

CAMP-MEETING AND GROUNDS

AT

WESLEYAN GROVE, MARTHA'S VINEYARD,

FOR THE ELEVEN YEARS ENDING WITH
THE MEETING OF 1869,

WITH GLANCES AT THE EARLIER YEARS.

BY

REV. H. VINCENT, A. M.,

AUTHOR OF "UNCONSCIOUS INFLUENCES," AND OF THE HISTORY
OF THIS MEETING TO 1858.

"Thou hast brought a vine out of Egypt; thou hast cast out the heathen, and planted it.
"Thou preparedst room before it, and didst cause it to take deep root, and it filled the land."
PSALM lxxx. 8, 9.

BOSTON:
LEE AND SHEPARD.
1870.

Entered, according to Act of Congress, in the year 1869, by
LEE AND SHEPARD,
In the Clerk's Office of the District Court of the District of Massachusetts.

STEREOTYPED AT THE
BOSTON STEREOTYPE FOUNDRY,
No. 19 Spring Lane.

PREFACE.

THE History of the Martha's Vineyard Camp-meeting, published some eleven years since, met with much favor. That History covered twenty-four years, and, including the meeting held at Westport Point in 1845, gave brief descriptions of twenty-four camp-meetings. These annual assemblages have been continued through an additional eleven years, and the writer of the former book has been repeatedly requested to furnish an account, in which the late wonderful changes in the exterior arrangements should be noted. Believing the appropriate time has arrived, he has finally decided to comply, and now offers the following volume, which he believes will be found to be as complete as the means of making such a work will allow. Such as it is, he commits it to the public, in the hope that it will help to remove existing prejudices against such gatherings generally, and thus promote those great interests to which the institution itself was designed to contribute.

The author takes pleasure in presenting the following cordial indorsement of this book by the Methodist clergymen of Boston: —

"*Resolved*, That we hear with great pleasure that Brother H. Vincent has prepared a history of Martha's Vineyard Camp-Meetings, and that we will commend it heartily to all those who are interested in that world-renowned Camp-Meeting."

CONTENTS.

CHAPTER		PAGE
	INTRODUCTION.— DESCRIPTION OF THE ISLAND.	9
I.	SKETCHES OF THE FIRST TWENTY-FOUR YEARS.	15
II.	CAMP-MEETING OF 1859, COMMENCING AUG. 9.	30
III.	" " 1860.	44
IV.	" " 1861.	63
V.	" " 1862.	83
VI.	" " 1863.	103
VII.	" " 1864.	115
VIII.	" " 1865.	131
IX.	" " 1866.	144
X.	" " 1867.	170
XI.	" " 1868.	196
XII.	" " 1869.	221

APPENDIX.

ACT OF INCORPORATION.	249
BY-LAWS.	251
LIST OF OFFICERS FOR 1869.	255
RULES OF THE CAMP-MEETING.	256
RESOLUTIONS.	258

DIRECTIONS TO VISITORS.

PERSONS from Boston and vicinity, wishing to visit the Camp-meeting Grounds, should take a New Bedford train, either from the Providence Railroad station, via Taunton, or the Old Colony Railroad station, via Fairhaven. These trains connect at New Bedford with the Vineyard steamer.

From Providence, Worcester, Hartford, and almost every other part of New England, they can make connections at the same point.

From New York, Brooklyn, and all places beyond, the route is by rail, or by steamer to Newport, Rhode Island, and then by rail to the steamer at New Bedford, Massachusetts, or by Portland steamer direct to the landings at the grounds.

INTRODUCTION.

IN a former work there was given in the Introduction a description of the location of the Wesleyan Grove and its surroundings; in this, as preliminary to what is to follow, it may be of some interest to note a few things respecting the island itself, which is the scene of the occurrences to be related, its business, and its resources.

Martha's Vineyard was discovered by Gosnold in the year 1602, about eighteen years before the landing at Plymouth, and was visited and settled by white men but a few years later than the last-named place. As on the main land, its native inhabitants have mostly disappeared, and the forests in which they roamed have, to a great extent, faded away under the hand of cultivation.

Some people singularly suppose that this island forms a part of Cape Cod.

It would seem unnecessary to state that the Vineyard, being an island, is no part of that cape, although it lies opposite to what may be properly called its head, or upper end. This island is a little less than twenty miles long; with the adjacent island of Chappaquiddic, which is usually regarded as an appendage, and, in great part, is parallel with it, it is twenty-one miles. Its greatest width is nine and a half miles; average width, five miles. At its nearest point it is about four miles from the main land, and from the city of New Bedford, by an air line, about twenty miles. From the same city to Edgartown, — situated on the eastern portion of the island, — it is about thirty miles distant. Located on the southern coast of the State of Massachusetts, it forms the south side of the Vineyard Sound, the great marine thoroughfare of this part of North America. On its northern and eastern sides the island is indented by bays and harbors, two of which harbors — Holmes Hole and Edgartown — are known as important to commercial interests. In the first named, immense fleets of vessels often stop for fair winds and tides, and the last is one of the safest and best harbors, in all winds and weather, on the coast.

The southern and eastern portions of the island are quite level, with, for the most part, a light, sandy soil, while the northern and western portions are hilly, rocky, and largely composed of heavy loam and various kinds of clay. There is some good farming land, especially in the western section. The southern and eastern portions seem to have been formed, in a remote antiquity of the world, by the wash of the ocean which bounded them; while it is probable the northern and western parts were, at some distant period of the long past, severed from the continent, and, having from that period endured the ever-wearing tides and waves, have contributed their share to the formation of the great marine highway before named. The south-eastern portions, also, which seem to have been similarly formed, are of late, by some strange counterforces of the same ocean, being washed way, and by the tides and waves formed into bars and shoals. Within the memory of those now living, nearly a quarter of a mile in width, for a distance of a dozen or more miles, has been lost to the island, small ponds being narrowed or wholly obliterated, and arable lands and meadows either covered with beach sand, or submerged by the force of the dashing sea. Near the shore as it extends around Chappaquiddic, where once were meadows, there is now a ship channel. But still the island stands, and doubtless will as long as the solid earth endures.

The lagoons, ponds, harbors, and surrounding waters of the island are very favorable for fishing; and there is but very little part of the year in which fish of various finny tribes cannot be obtained by the hardy inhabitants. The facilities for boating, the cooling sea breezes, the pleasant drives, and comfortable state of the atmosphere at night, even in the heated term, — all contribute to render it an exceedingly desirable summer retreat. Of the attractions of the island, in addition to those just glanced at, allusion needs only to be made to the view of the boundless expanse of the blue ocean, and the dashing of the waves at the " South Shore," and the varied-colored cliffs of the ever-proudly towering Gay Head.

The principal business of the island has been that of whaling. The late rebellion, as it is well known, made sad inroads here, as elsewhere, upon this branch of maritime adventure; but the people are now beginning, in some small measure, to renew investments in the same occupation. May God save us and the country at large forever hereafter from the pirates of our own shores, and from the treachery of the fatherland!

Sources of wealth lie embedded in vast masses beneath the surface, especially in the north-western parts of the island. Reference is here made to the various kinds of clay found there. For many years clays for mechanical purposes have been exported, in considerable quantities, both from Gay Head and from other localities along the Sound Shore. There has also long been a brick-yard established at a place called the "Roaring Brook." But the extent and value of the mines of mineral wealth here have been but partially known and estimated, till within a few years past. After various ownerships, and the acquisition of very considerable tracts by purchase, the brick-yard, with the added premises, has lately passed into the hands of Hon. Nathaniel Harris, of Brookline, at a cost of fifty-five thousand dollars. The establishment bears the title of the "Vineyard Brick and Tile Works." The formation of the brick is now done by steam power. Eighty-five tons of clay and sand are used *per diem*, making about sixty bricks per minute, and about thirty thousand per day. The kiln department can contain one million bricks duly piled for burning. Clays are also exported from different wharves along the shore. As an additional index to the varieties of mineral wealth existing here, there is, a mile or two distant from the establishment above named, a Paint Mill on a large scale, and still farther north-easterly an establishment by a Peat Company.

On this island of the ocean, — thus hastily and imperfectly described, — near what is known as the East

Chop or Bluff of Holmes Hole harbor, from which site are fine views of the water, fleets of vessels, and neighboring towns, is the justly-celebrated Wesleyan Grove, in which, at convenient times for thirty-four summers, the Methodists, with many of other denominations, have assembled to offer their devotions to God, and to put forth special efforts for the advancement of His cause.

The grove, as a suitable location for holding a camp-meeting, was first brought to notice by the late Jeremiah Pease, Esq. The place for the stand was selected by four or five brethren of Edgartown, of whom the writer of this book alone survives.

HISTORY

OF THE

Camp-meeting at Wesleyan Grove.

CHAPTER I.

SKETCHES OF THE FIRST TWENTY-FOUR YEARS.

THE first camp-meeting held here was in the year 1835, commencing August 24. The ground had been leased, and a portion of it cleared of underbrush. A rough shed was erected for the preachers' stand, the interior of which was their lodging-room, rye straw being furnished for their bedding. Fortunate was he of the "cloth" who could get an extra bundle for his pillow. The seats for the audience were of plain, rough boards, without backs. The entire area cleared was small, and but nine tents graced the circle. Some of these were quite rudely constructed. A few hundred people attended; probably not over a thousand heard preaching at any one time. The Presiding Elder of the District being unable to be present, Rev. Thomas C. Pierce, since deceased, was chosen to superintend. It was an excellent meeting; the number of converts reported was sixty-five.

The meeting of 1836 commenced August 22. In the absence of the Presiding Elder, Rev. James C. Boutecou was chosen Superintendent. Some additional improvements had been made upon the grounds. Good order was maintained. The work of grace was mostly in the church and among backsliders, many of the latter being reclaimed. About twenty were converted. Among the preachers of this year were Revs. Phineas Crandall, Shipley W. Willson, and David Leslie, the last-named afterward a missionary to the "Flat Head Indians" beyond the Rocky Mountains.

1837. The meeting commenced Monday, August 14, and was held, as it had been the two years previous, between Sabbaths. Who presided does not now appear. Rev. Phineas

Crandall was the Secretary. One of the most prominent of the preachers was the venerable Asa Kent, since deceased. The number of tents had increased to twelve. The number of ministers present was seventeen, and the largest congregation was thought to number two thousand. The number of conversions was about the same as the year preceding.

1838. The meeting this year commenced Wednesday, August 28, and held over the Sabbath. The Presiding Elder was present, and preached one of the sermons. Revs. F. Upham, J. T. Burrell, and A. Kent were also among the number who preached. Rev. Franklin Fisk gave a report of the meeting for Zion's Herald. Converts about twenty. Glowing descriptions of the grove and of the meetings were published in these early years.

1839. The fifth of the series commenced on the 14th day of August, and held over the Sabbath. The number of tents had increased to seventeen. Including the Presiding Elder there were twenty-six ministers in attendance. Rev. Jared Perkins of the New Hampshire Conference, Rev. John Allen of Maine, — known as

"Camp-meeting John Allen," — and Rev. John Adams, — styled "Reformation John Adams," — and the venerable Daniel Webb, and Isaac Bonney, were among the preachers on the occasion. Rev. S. W. Coggeshall was the Secretary.

1840. The Committee appointed for the purpose the preceding year, obtained a new lease for five years. The names of that Committee were, Thomas M. Coffin, Isaiah D. Pease, and Jeremiah Pease. The meeting commenced August 10. Rev. Bartholomew Otheman, the Presiding Elder, was present, and had charge of the exercises. It was at one of the business meetings this year that this grove received the name of "Wesleyan Grove." Quite a number were converted, several of them after the regular camp-meeting services were concluded.

1841. Rev. B. Otheman was again Superintendent. The celebrated temperance lecturer John W. Hawkins was present, and addressed about three thousand people on Sabbath afternoon. At all these camp-meetings it was customary to have, at some time, a Love Feast and the Sacrament. Isaiah D. Pease, Esq., Sheriff of the County, was appointed Committee of Arrangements for the ensuing year.

1842. The meeting began on August 17, and was under the same Superintendent, Rev. B. Otheman. The plan of the preceding year, of having two Secretaries, — one for the records, and another for reporting the meeting for the Herald, — was continued. Rev. Charles S. McReading was one of the two this year.

1843, August 9. It is not now certainly known who was the president of this meeting, but it is thought to have been the Rev. B. Otheman, then Presiding Elder of the New Bedford District. Rev. David Patten was reporting secretary. The subject of preserving the Sabbath inviolate was much discussed at the meetings of the preachers and tent-masters; and a Committee, consisting of A. U. Swinerton, H. Vincent, and J. Lovejoy, was appointed to address our community on this subject. The number of conversions is not now definitely known, but was quite large.

1844. The meeting began on Wednesday, August the 21st. This was the tenth held in this beautiful grove. Rev. F. Upham, of the New Bedford District, was our Superintendent. Rev. A. H. Newton preached the first sermon.

The second was by the venerable Lewis Bates, since gone to his rest. Among the ministers in attendance was Rev. Brother House, of New Bedford, who was "in labors abundant." Connected with this meeting, which was a good one, is cherished the remembrance of the timely conversion, among others, of Abraham Lewis, of Edgartown, who retired early from the camp, and died suddenly, ere the tent's company had arrived home. Whether wisely or not, it was decided to discontinue the camp-meetings here, and go to some other location. The fixtures were disposed of, and Rev. F. Upham was chosen a committee to fix on a site for holding a meeting the following year.

1845. The place fixed upon was Westport Point, in the County of Bristol, in this state. Rev. F. Upham was President, and H. Vincent Secretary. Noble men were there. The names of such heralds as Isaac Bonney, Daniel Webb, J. S. House, and Charles Pitman, D. D., live in history, and in the affections of many hearts. Dr. Pitman was the great preacher of the occasion. He not only preached here, but also on the steamer on her return trip to New Bedford.

John Wilde, a superior singer, was there from Duxbury. It was a large gathering; but the difficulties attending the approach to the place by water, and some other considerations, led to the determination not to hold another meeting there. It was voted to hold two camp-meetings the next year, one at East Greenwich, R. I., and another at Wareham, Mass. The parting scene here was, as usual, quite affecting.

1846. The meeting was held, as agreed upon, at East Greenwich, with favorable results. On examination it was thought inexpedient to hold the meeting at Wareham, or vicinity. There being some delay for consultation, and no other site being recommended as eligible, the Methodist Church in Edgartown, in consultation with Rev. B. Otheman, Presiding Elder of the new Sandwich District, requested him to appoint a camp-meeting at the Wesleyan Grove, which he did. Brother Sirson P. Coffin, by appointment of the Quarterly Methodist Conference of this church, obtained of the proprietors a lease of these lands for five years, to hold camp-meetings. A new stand and seats were constructed, and all preliminaries duly arranged.

Rev. F. Upham presided, and Rev. D. Patten, Jr. was the Secretary. Prayer and praise were again heard in this Grove. Dr. C. Pitman was with us. There were some twelve or fifteen converts and a general quickening.

1847. This meeting commenced on Monday, August 23, and closed on the following Saturday. Rev. F. Upham again presided. The venerable Daniel Fillmore and John W. Hardy were present at this meeting. The good results of such a meeting cannot be enumerated in a single paragraph; but among them was the conversion of about thirty persons.

The meeting for 1848 commenced August 8. Rev. Thomas Ely, who succeeded Mr. Upham on the New Bedford District, presided. The sermons were by Revs. E. Grant, J. E. Gifford, W. Richards, W. Cone, J. Cady, R. W. Allen, T. Hardman, J. Livesey, D. Webb, J. Lovejoy, Robert Allyn, W. Livesey, H. Baylies, C. H. Titus, R. Livesey, F. Upham, N. Goodrich, S. W. Coggeshall, and H. W. Houghton. There were about forty conversions. Father Webb, who had been in the ministry about fifty years, was requested to preach his semi-centennial sermon the next year.

1849. The meeting commenced on the 20th of August, holding between Sabbaths. Rev. T. Ely was again Superintendent. Sirson P. Coffin was Chairman of the Committee of Arrangements. He was authorized to obtain a lease of the ground at reasonable rates for ten years. All expenses were met. A new well was ordered to be dug. The place seemed, if possible, more delightful than ever before. Here were ministers of different ages — the young soldier, the men of middle life full of vigor, and the venerable fathers with silvered locks and furrowed cheeks. The names of Webb, Bates, Otis, Hardy, and others are, and will remain, historical. The first named, in accordance with the vote of the preceding year, delivered his semi-centennial address. There were, in all, about fifty tents. It was computed that about fifty persons were converted, fifteen of them after the sermon of the last evening.

1850. Rev. T. Ely was again in charge. Among others who preached were Webb, Burnham, Atwater, Otheman, Hobart. The meeting was larger than ever before. There were of all classes eighty-seven tents. Many professors of religion experienced a deepening of the work of grace, and it was estimated that, in the judgment of charity, one hundred were converted. The place was the admiration of strangers, many of whom were in attendance. Mr. Coffin had obtained the ten years' lease. The yearly rent, as stipulated, was thirty dollars. A Committee on Improvements, of which Preston Bennet, Esq. was Chairman, was appointed. They afterward reported through Rev. B. Otheman, recommending the new seating of the ground, and the providing of other additional fixtures.

1851. Rev. Mr. Ely, of the New Bedford District, presided for the fourth time. Jeremiah Pease, Sen. was reappointed Chorister, having acted in that capacity for many years. There were, of all sorts, about one hundred tents, and, by estimation, between three thousand five hundred and four thousand people in the congregation on the Sabbath. The weather was very fine most of the time. The introductory sermon was by Father Bates. There were sixty ministers present. Thirty-four persons professed conversion; among them an aged sea captain, living in the vicinity, and owning much land.

He was then in his last sickness. He died soon after, and went, we trust, to better possessions above.

1852. Rev. Pardon T. Kenney, of the Sandwich District, and Rev. David Patten, Jr., of the Providence District, were both present. Mr. Patten was chosen the Superintendent of this meeting. A Committee on "Order" was appointed, of which Jeremiah Pease, Sen. was Chairman. The Finance Committee was reconstructed. Joseph Brownell, of New Bedford, was the Chairman. New tents were added. In all there were now about one hundred and forty-five. There were about sixty ministers present. Those of other denominations than the Methodist were always reckoned in. It will be seen that here, as elsewhere, there was *progress*. This is a univeral law. This was one of the most wonderful meetings of the series. There were reckoned to be one hundred and forty conversions.

1853. Rev. D. Patten, Jr., Presiding Elder of the Providence District, was again chosen to preside. Love and Harmony prevailed. Dr. and Mrs. Palmer were present; also that well-known philanthropist, Deacon Moses Grant, of Boston. Notwithstanding the improvements made, still others were ordered. "Jesus received sinners still."

1854. Rev. Pardon T. Kenney, Presiding Elder of the Sandwich District, presided over this meeting. There was some increase in the numbers in attendance. The sermons were able, and the meeting interesting. Present, Rev. B. W. Gorham, of the Wyoming Conference, Samuel Norris, of New Hampshire, and R. W. Allen and H. V. Degen, of the New England.

Voted, in one of the business meetings, that the two Presiding Elders of the Providence and Sandwich Districts should preside alternately over this meeting. Captain William B. Lawton and Dr. Stevens, both of Providence, were chosen Choristers. It was voted to enlarge the main circle, so as to admit two more tents.

1855. This meeting commenced August 21, and closed on the 28th. Dr. Roberts, of Baltimore, was present, and preached. There were now two hundred tents. Rev. Charles H. Titus, Presiding Elder of the Providence District, presided. The Vigilance Committee were prompt in the enforcement of the rules. Sirson P. Coffin was the agent of the meeting. Henry Bradley, of Holmes Hole, was the Treasurer. The question of holding the camp-meetings over the Sabbath was again discussed, and the two Presiding Elders were requested to consult their several societies on the subject.

The meeting of 1856 commenced August 14. Rev. Paul Townsend, Presiding Elder of the Sandwich District, whose turn it was to preside, being absent, Rev. Mr. Titus, of the Providence District, was chosen to fill his place. Rev. John F. Wright, of Ohio, late Book Agent at Cincinnati, was present, and preached; also Rev. John N. Coombs, of Alexandria, a member of the Baltimore Conference. Father Wright represented the Colored People's College in Ohio. There were about seventy ministers present. This year, for the first time, a tax of fifty cents was laid upon each tent, great and small, to aid in defraying the expense of the meeting. Alonzo Smith, of Holmes Hole, was appointed Agent.

1857. The meeting commenced August 20. Many friends were on the ground this year quite in advance of the time of beginning. There were in all about two hundred and fifty tents, the larger portion, of course, family tents. Sixty ministers were present. Rev. Paul Townsend, of the Sandwich District, although he had just come from Eastham, where he presided, entered upon a similar responsibility here. The number of conversions was about fifty, among them that of a young Jew, who has since become a preacher. There were also several other young men of promise converted to Christ.

1858. The premises, including the camp-meeting site, having been sold by the owners last year, subject to the lease, they were reconveyed to the old owners during the year preceding this meeting. Rev. P. Townsend was again chosen President, with Rev. C. H. Titus as his Assistant. H. Vincent was reappointed Secretary, while Rev. W. Richards was to report the meeting for the Herald and Journal. Great numbers were in attendance, very many, doubtless, prompted to come by the great religious awakening in the country the preceding year. Notwithstanding the immense masses, excellent order prevailed.

Many distinguished strangers visited the place during this meeting, among them His Excellency Governor Nathaniel P. Banks, and Rev. Thomas Brainard, D. D., a prominent Presbyterian clergyman from Philadelphia. About twenty persons were converted. About sixty lots for new tents next year were engaged. Still greater improvements were designed.

These brief glances at the years covered by the volume written by the author, and published by Rev. A. B. Wheeler, in 1858, are given to help the conceptions of the reader of the following chapters, and also for the purpose of calling attention to that volume, in which the meetings of those years are so fully described. All who would have the complete History of the Encampment from the beginning, should procure that work, which is still for sale at the low price at which it was at first published.

CHAPTER II.

CAMP-MEETING OF 1859, COMMENCING AUG. 9.

THIS year seemed to inaugurate a new era in the history of this encampment, and affords, therefore, a very proper beginning of this added volume of reminiscences. For the sake of accuracy, however, it must be stated that important incipient measures were adopted the preceding year, which culminated in this. The meeting having increased from year to year in the numbers attending it, larger and more substantial accommodations were now required. Already, as may have been seen in the description of the doings of the previous year, small wooden buildings, in a few instances, had taken the places of tents. These were indices of increased confidence in the permanence of the meetings in this location. Among the new fixtures of the place, were additional means

Many distinguished strangers visited the place during this meeting, among them His Excellency Governor Nathaniel P. Banks, and Rev. Thomas Brainard, D. D., a prominent Presbyterian clergyman from Philadelphia. About twenty persons were converted. About sixty lots for new tents next year were engaged. Still greater improvements were designed.

These brief glances at the years covered by the volume written by the author, and published by Rev. A. B. Wheeler, in 1858, are given to help the conceptions of the reader of the following chapters, and also for the purpose of calling attention to that volume, in which the meetings of those years are so fully described. All who would have the complete History of the Encampment from the beginning, should procure that work, which is still for sale at the low price at which it was at first published.

CHAPTER II.

CAMP-MEETING OF 1859, COMMENCING AUG. 9.

THIS year seemed to inaugurate a new era in the history of this encampment, and affords, therefore, a very proper beginning of this added volume of reminiscences. For the sake of accuracy, however, it must be stated that important incipient measures were adopted the preceding year, which culminated in this. The meeting having increased from year to year in the numbers attending it, larger and more substantial accommodations were now required. Already, as may have been seen in the description of the doings of the previous year, small wooden buildings, in a few instances, had taken the places of tents. These were indices of increased confidence in the permanence of the meetings in this location. Among the new fixtures of the place, were additional means of supplying to the encampment an abundance of pure water. There had also been erected the substantial wooden building previously contemplated, as a kind of headquarters of the encampment. This building was placed at a little distance from the main circle, near what was then the main entrance to the ground, and near the foot of what is now Trinity Park. It is twenty-four by forty feet, two and a half stories high, and has several apartments, adapted to the varied wants, viz.: A large room for the storage of stray baggage, and as a place for general deposit, and in one corner of which a post-office was kept, *pro tem.*; another smaller room, nicely finished and furnished, as an office for the agent; another, devoted to lanterns and oil, and to the work of preparing the means of lighting the tents and the camp. In the second story is the Agent's lodging-room, the Finance Committee's room, and a large room sufficient to seat a hundred or more persons, in which were to be held the general business meetings of the ministers and tent-masters, and other officers of the encampment. The attic might be used for a lodging-room for strangers, and during the year for the deposit of tent-covers and other goods. Strange as it may now seem, this building was put up at an expense of a little less than a thousand dollars.

Other and extensive improvements had been made on the grounds. Immediately in the rear of the main circle — the circle of large tents — had been laid out and prepared, an avenue forty feet in width, encompassing the entire circle. All carts, baggage wagons, and carriages designed to approach this circle were required to take this wide avenue, instead of entering the area, which was forbidden during the continuance of the camp-meeting and for a while previously thereto. Besides the annoyance thus prevented, this wide, open street made what were then the rear parts of the grounds much more airy and pleasant, many of the smaller tents having been moved back to the outer line of this thoroughfare. This main avenue was at first named Asbury Avenue, commemorative of one of the first bishops of the Methodist Episcopal Church, but the name was afterward changed to that of Broadway. One of the smaller avenues, branching off from the above, was called Fisk

Avenue, in memory of that most excellent scholar and divine, whose praise is in all the churches. This name has not been superseded. May it never be! There had been many of these smaller avenues laid out, and, like the main one, cleared of underbrush and litter. There had also been cleared up, in what was then the southern part of the encampment, a nice park, first called Coke's Park, after the great missionary apostle, some time the co-laborer in the episcopacy with the venerable Asbury, but afterward changed to the more popular name of Trinity Park. Among other great conveniences provided was a bell, of considerable size, placed near the ministers' stand, to be used to announce the hours for public service, and those of rising in the morning and retiring at night.

Many of the churches in this section of New England, for their convenience as companies, and individual gentlemen, — members and others, — for the comfort of themselves and friends, were not a whit behind the managers of the meeting in their arrangements and preparations. More or less of this work had been in progress for a month or two previous. Several large new tents for companies had been located, and over a hundred new ones, of smaller sizes, had been put up in different parts of the grove.* Some of these had been fitted up at considerable cost, and with much taste.

Those who had been so much accustomed to camp-meeting scenes, and especially to the varying aspects of the meetings here, for a quarter of a century nearly, were quite astonished at the extent and village-like appearances of this encampment. To see streets (called here avenues) of houses — temporary though they were — was wholly unusual at the places of such gatherings. The weather at the beginning was beautiful, and as quite a collection of people had already assembled, the grove was vocal with prayer and praise. The beauty and loveliness of an evening view of the encampment, with its hundreds of tents lighted up, are seldom exceeded by anything in the world's panorama. This, of itself, would richly repay a visit to the place. The Rev. Dr. Parks, who was on a visit here from the State of New York, gave it as his opinion, that it was

* The steamer brought the frames for about forty such tents in a single day.

then the largest meeting of the kind in the world: for, so far as known, such meetings are not held out of this country, and this was evidently the largest in America. This year it promised to be, as usual, the mammoth campmeeting. With the people who came some days before the commencement of the meeting, came also a few of the ministers, so that sermons were delivered on the Sabbath.

The first regular public service of this camp-meeting was held at the stand on the evening of the 9th of August, the day appointed. A well-adapted sermon was delivered by Rev. Charles H. Titus, of Warren, R. I. He counselled us to "inquire for the old paths, and to walk therein."

The person chosen to superintend this camp-meeting was the Rev. George M. Carpenter, then Presiding Elder of the Providence District.

On the following day, which was Wednesday, sermons were preached by Revs. Henry S. White, of Newport, R. I., H. H. Hartwell, of the New Hampshire Conference, and E. K. Colby. On Thursday we had able sermons by Rev. Dr. Parks, of the Oneida Conference, Rev.

William McDonald, of Providence, and Rev. Samuel W. Coggeshall, of Taunton. They were all well calculated to promote the great and holy objects of the meeting. On Friday, the fourth day, Rev. Frederick Upham, who travelled the circuit of this island with the venerable Francis Dane, some thirty-four or thirty-five years before, Rev. J. A. M. Chapman, of Chestnut Street Church, Providence, and Rev. Gilbert Haven, of Cambridge, were the preachers. The sermons of the afternoon and evening were followed by other interesting exercises.

The weather was still fine, but very dry, and the roads, consequently, very dusty.

Among the many visiting the ground, there were, about this time, some suspicious-looking persons; but we had, as usual, a strong police force out both by day and by night, and a regiment of volunteers might have been raised very speedily, had there been occasion for it. Nothing, however, occurred to mar the general peace. As our people were for peace with all men, and would gladly have persuaded all who came there to be at peace with their God, so we trusted, that, although evil-disposed persons might visit the place as they do other localities, we should be kept unharmed.

At this stage of the meeting the steamer Eagle's Wing was making two trips a day from New Bedford, and the steamer Island Home was daily visiting these waters from Nantucket and Hyannis. Crowds were also arriving by other conveyances, and some five thousand, or more, people thronged the grove. There was room for all, and many more.

On Saturday morning there was a refreshing rain. It was, of course, very acceptable. It laid the dust, and cooled the air; and we felt that we ought to be grateful for this, as for all other blessings. Its effect, among other good things, was to make people more sociable, and, by invigorating the mind as well as the body, prepare us for more energetic endeavors for the furtherance of the Master's cause.

The weather continuing wet, there was no public preaching at the stand during the day; but, as usual on such occasions, there were sermons, delivered at the stated hours, in several of the larger tents. There was also much of prayer and praise. On every other day of this meeting the weather was favorable for out-of-door preaching.

On the Sabbath the customary camp-meeting Love Feast was held at the stand at eight o'clock. The preaching of the day was by Rev. L. D. Davis, of Edgartown, and Revs. J. B. Gould, and A. McKeown, both of Fall River. The numbers in and about the grounds on this, the great day of the meeting, were estimated to be about twelve thousand — the same as the preceding year.

The sermons on Monday were by Rev. Messrs. Hannaford, of Lynn, Latham, of Holmes Hole, and Cushman, of Charlestown.

Ordinarily, the camp-meeting here holds about a week. This year the experiment was tried of adding two or three extra days.

Tuesday. At eight o'clock this morning, the Sacrament of the Lord's Supper was administered. There was preaching by Rev. Mr. Mead, of the Five Points Mission, in New York, Rev. Samuel F. Upham, of Pawtucket, R. I., and Rev. James D. Butler, of the Seamen's Bethel, New Bedford. "Friend" Joseph Tillinghast, of New Bedford, who takes great delight in addressing children, and making them little presents, was here at this time, and, at a suitable hour, talked to the little folks in his usual happy way.

The people were still coming and going, and among the visitors were the Hon. Oliver Warner, Secretary of State, Hon. John Morissey, Sergeant at Arms, Hon. Isaac O. Barnes, late United States Marshal, and numerous other distinguished gentlemen. It was stated that Governor Banks was intending to come, but the disastrous fire at the State Reform School for Boys, at Westboro', required his attention there.

On Wednesday the preaching was by Revs. John Howson, F. S. De Hass, of New York, and John E. Gifford.

On Thursday, the last day of the meeting, there were sermons by Rev. Charles Nason, of New Bedford Pleasant Street Church, and by Rev. William Livesey. At the closing service, in the evening, the audience were addressed by the President of the meeting, Rev. Mr. Carpenter, and by Rev. Messrs. Townsend, Titus, Hamblen, and Richards, and also by several laymen, not the least of whom was our veritable friend John C. Scott, Esq., of Millville, Chief of the Night Police, whose shrill voice, echoing through the grove at the evening hour of "ten o'clock," will never be forgotten.

During this camp-meeting there were present, more or less of the time, by actual enumeration, over one hundred clergymen of different denominations, most of them Methodists, of course. The tents of the encampment were not very accurately counted, but it was judged there were, of all kinds, more than four hundred. The whole expense of preparing the grounds this year, so far as it was a general cost, was found to be about sixteen hundred dollars, most of which was paid.

The sermons at this camp-meeting were well constructed and well delivered. Some of them were rather too decidedly doctrinal for such an occasion, but many others were of the true revival stamp. The spiritual traits of the meeting were an improvement upon those of the preceding year. About thirty persons professed conversion, some of them of very good social position in the communities in which they resided.

During much of the time, an artist was present from New Bedford, taking stereoscopic views of different tents, with their occupants, and of different sections and scenes.

To the account of this camp-meeting, thus given, I add the following outside view, from the Boston Atlas and Bee, which, although not absolutely correct in all its figures, will be found interesting : —

"NEW BEDFORD, August 16.

"This is the season of the year when the Methodists enjoy their annual religious festival, under the term of camp-meeting, which implies a meeting of a multitude in camp or tents.

"I have just returned from the great meeting now so popular in Holmes Hole. It was, to me, an extraordinary show, as I. had never before seen anything of the kind.

"I have seen thirty thousand soldiers in camp, have seen them drilled for effective military duty, but this display of men, women, and children in their own tents, which have been erected with much taste, furnished so neatly, and many of them with all the luxuries of a city drawing-room (like Colonel Hatch's elegant college-built tent, of Hatch, Gray & Co's. Boston Express, and also Mr. Edward Monro's, of Davenport, Monro & Co's., Express), — I say that this extraordinary sight, beneath green forest trees, may well astonish any person.

"When I first visited the encampment on Sunday last, there were, probably, twenty thousand persons assembled within a circuit of three miles; and, although the day was the blessed Sabbath, the scene, for a few hours, reminded me of the Fourth of July, minus fireworks and boisterousness. Everybody appeared happy, joyful, smiling; thousands of young and beautiful females, elegantly dressed, promenaded along green paths with young men, whilst an immense crowd listened attentively to eloquent and deeply impressive addresses from clergymen, whose only object appeared to be to save souls.

"Many thousand persons visited the camp-meeting merely to enjoy a day's pleasure, and seemed to take not the slightest interest in the religious services; but not one individual interfered in any manner to interrupt or disturb the true worshippers beneath the bright-silver-and blue canopy of heaven. There was a sacred circle of Christians within the great outside crowd, from whence went up to the great God fervent prayers from the heart, and great and ever-living biblical truths.

"I speak of the *tout ensemble* as an extraordinary show. I never before saw a finer display of beautiful women, better regularity, or thousands so well conducting themselves, as at this camp ground.

"This religious festival is, to the Methodists, like a Newport or Saratoga, without the great bustle, fashion, ceremony, and expense of such places, while the pure elements of religion are included by them as an additional luxury and enjoyment.

"I am happy to add that several 'awful' hard sinners have been converted.

"This city has been crowded with strangers during the last few days, and on several occasions, in the large dining-room at the Parker House, beds were placed on the floor, to accommodate the rush of strangers.

"The fine steamer Eagle's Wing, Captain Cromwell, has been crowded every trip for ten days.

"C. H. P."

CHAPTER III.

CAMP-MEETING OF 1860.

THIS meeting commenced its regular public services at the stand, on Tuesday evening, August 21. Such, however, had been the numbers rusticating here previously, that preaching was enjoyed on the Sabbath preceding. Even then this preliminary season of rustication, so extensive and long-continued in later years, had become quite a favorite idea with many who could spare the time. But the custom, although not yet very pervading, elicited discussion and opposition. Some good people had come to think that the religious character of our gatherings here had very much changed of late years, and that the rustic and social antepast had much to do with the wanings of spirituality at our camp-meetings. There was therefore this year an earnest effort put forth by many, both of the ministry and laity, who had the vital interests at heart, to revive the old standards of effectiveness in Christian labor, with a view to the attaining of the successes of other years.

The first sermon was by Rev. L. D. Davis, of Edgartown, founded on Isaiah lxvi. 6. It was what was needed, and was listened to with interest. We felt, on leaving the seats, more deeply than when we assembled, the responsibilities under which we rested.

On the following days of the meeting, owing to the frequent and heavy rains, public preaching at the stand was not so regular as in some other years. When thus prevented from occupying the public seats, we had, as is customary at such times, preaching by several ministers at the same hour, in some of the large society-tents. This may have been favorable to the general spirituality, and other good results, inasmuch as it brought into requisition the talents and earnest labors of a larger number of ministers, concentrated in working sections the members of the churches, and brought in under the influence of Christian effort many persons who else would have been needlessly promenading, or otherwise idling away their time. But we were also blessed with some good weather, and on those days, and parts of days, we had some excellent sermons from the stand.

On the second day, Wednesday, there was a sermon in the afternoon by Rev. David H. Ela, of Bristol, R. I., and in the evening by Rev. James D. Butler, of the Seamen's Bethel, New Bedford.

On Thursday there was preaching in the forenoon by Rev. Samuel C. Brown, of Providence. In the afternoon Rev. Seth Reed, of Detroit, Mich., preached a powerful discourse from Luke xxiv. 26. Theme, "The results of the sufferings of Christ upon the government of God and the destinies of man." The topics discussed were very lucidly and instructively presented. Rev. Henry S. White, of Newport, R. I., was the preacher of the evening.

On Friday the only service at the stand was in the evening. The sermon was by Rev. Merritt P. Alderman.

On Saturday there was preaching in the forenoon by Rev. W. H. Black, of Kentucky, — a true man, — a member of the last preceding general conference, and in the evening by Rev. Charles Nason, of New Bedford.

Sunday was a fine day, and, as usual, — so far at least as attendance is concerned, — the great day of the meeting. The sermon at ten o'clock was one of power. It was by Rev. Sidney Dean, of Pawtucket, R. I., on "The vine and the branches." In the afternoon Rev. S. Reed, of Detroit, addressed us again, in thrilling strains, on "The law of the Lord is perfect, converting the soul." Rev. J. A. M. Chapman, of Providence, occupied the stand in the evening. Besides these, there were several sermons at out-posts, by other ministers, at hours not interfering with these stated appointments. It was counselled that if our numbers increase, and especially of such as will not come to the accustomed place of worship, we should put forth corresponding exertions, follow them out to their places of concourse and resort, and address them there, thus endeavoring to reach all.

On Monday, Rev. Joseph Marsh, of Sandwich, Rev. Charles H. Payne, of East Bridgewater, and Rev. William McDonald, of Providence, were the preachers.

On Tuesday, the last day of the meeting, the sermons were by Rev. William H. Richards, of Newport, R. I., Rev. John W. Willet, of Wareham, and Rev. Charles H. Titus, of Warren, R. I.

Some of the special occasions of this camp-meeting worthy of note were, the address to the children on Friday, by Father Tillinghast, and the Love Feast on Sabbath morning, at which about one hundred persons spoke, including ministers and members of other denominations. On Monday morning over five hundred persons, including about thirty ministers, participated in the sacred communion of the Lord's Supper. The prayer-meetings at the stand were but few, but they were seasons of special interest. The prayer-meetings in the large tents, at hours designated, were also spiritual, and held with special promptness. The Presiding Elder said that in one instance there were thirty-six of these, by actual count, all in action, and when the time to close arrived, in five minutes after he struck the bell, all had ceased.

Preparatory to this meeting, additional improvements had been made. The new and beautiful cottages, although the number was still small, were objects of great attraction. The most costly and beautiful of these was that of Perez Mason and William B. Lawton, at the head of Trinity Park. Four or five new society tents had been erected; among the number, one had been placed in the circle through the efforts of Rev. J. D. Butler, for the accommodation of his parishioners, the seamen, and styled the " Bethel Tent." About one hundred other tents had been added, mostly for families, but a few on a large scale, for boarding. About this time many tents, both large and small, were made with board sides and cloth tops. It might seem to the uninitiated that at these camp-meetings we have too many religious exercises during the day, and that we are thus too constantly taxed with these duties for our own profit, even. This may be true with regard to some not possessing health; but such need not attend all unless they choose. As to others, having laid aside our home cares for the express purpose of attending these services, we can, for one week at least, bear a little more than the usual strain upon mind and heart. Then, again, the interest we feel in the work adds, temporarily, to the powers of endurance.

The general religious character of this meeting was decidedly better than for several years. The object for which many had preached, prayed, and labored, that the religious element might predominate, had been realized. There had been quite a number of conversions.

Among the visitors here was "Camp-meeting John Allen," who was converted at a camp-meeting, and had since attended over a hundred such meetings. On this, as on other occasions, he rendered good service. There were also present a number of gentlemen of the Press, and among them *he* who is called "*Mrs.* Partington."

Some of the incidents of the weather were as follows: On Friday night a very high wind accompanied the rain, blowing down the North Bridgewater boarding-tent, and injuring several others. During one other night we had a heavy rain, accompanied with lightning and thunder. It came up very suddenly. The day had been one of the most serene we had enjoyed. At half past ten o'clock in the evening there was a clear sky, and a brilliant moon was riding in splendor through the heavens. At a little past midnight we were resting under one of the heaviest thunder-storms of the season. With the morning came the bright sun.

At a business-meeting on Thursday of the camp-meeting week, the agent, Sirson P. Coffin, Esq., read from manuscript his annual report, — which was elaborate, — in which he recommended a new organization of our business affairs. It was proposed that instead of the method heretofore pursued, we form an association composed of those persons who then constituted our business-meetings, thus inaugurating more of system and securing greater permanence. One feature of the plan was to commit the entire police regulations and the general financial matters to a large committee of laymen, thus relieving the ministers and tent-masters from much care, and giving them more opportunity for specific Christian labors. The report was highly acceptable, and was adopted with great unanimity. It was ordered to be printed, together with a series of regulations, and the rules of the camp-meeting.

To show somewhat of the progress of this encampment since the return of the meeting from Westport Point, in the year 1846, I give here some extracts from the report itself.

"In 1846 there were thirteen societies and one family tent. The expense that year, including speakers' stand, seats, pump, &c., amounted to one hundred and seventy-five dollars; and even this small amount was a standing debt against the concern for three years, before the money could be raised to cancel it. After the first year, the expenses for three years did not exceed seventy-five dollars, and there were upon an average from fifty to one hundred conversions each year.

"What a change has come over the nature of these meetings! Here, beneath the shade of the stately oak, surrounded on one side by the broad Atlantic, on the other by the Vineyard Sound, while stretched across, and looming up with neat little cottages and spires, stand Holmes Hole Village, Falmouth, and Edgartown,— here, on this secluded spot, where Nature and Nature's God inspire the higher thoughts of man, and lift him above the things of earth, are thousands reposing, who once in a year retire from the busy cares of the world, and pay their vows in song and praise to God for his goodness.

" Here, where one hundred and fifty, with their fifteen little tents, used to toil day by day, many times wet and poorly provided for, now stand the cottages and the little palaces, which we can enumerate by hundreds, as cosily and securely provided with conveniences as any city home can boast of. Where seventy-five to one hundred and fifty dollars used to pay the expenses of the week's encampment, now, we were about to say, almost as many thousands are spent annually for the enjoyment of a week.

" Then, when the one-horse team and the little skiff were used to convey them hither in close proximity around, now the iron-horse thunders them on and over the bay from every quarter of New England! How things have changed! Who can consider the rapid strides of the wisdom of God in man?"

Following the report of the Agent, there was read by the Secretary, at the Agent's request, and by consent of the meeting, a set of " Articles of Agreement," or constitution, offered to the meeting for adoption in the organization of the new association. They were acted upon, item by item, and, after some slight alterations, adopted.

Article I. fixed the name of the association to be the "Martha's Vineyard Camp-meeting Association."

Article II. defined the membership of the Association.

Article III. gave direction as to who should officiate from time to time as the President of the Association.

Article IV. provided for certain other officers, and prescribed the times at which they should be chosen.

Article V. assigned to the Presiding Officer, the Secretary, Treasurer, and Agent of the meeting, such duties as customarily devolve upon like officers.

Article VI. prescribed the method by which the large Finance Committee, consisting of fifteen laymen, should be chosen; and

Article VII. defined their duties and responsibilities.

Article VIII., under three sections, marked out the duties of the agent of the meeting.

Article IX. required a yearly report on financial matters.

Article X. says, "All powers, prerogatives,

and privileges, not herein expressly delegated to the said Finance Committee, are reserved by this Association, which shall from time to time adopt such measures and enact such regulations for the government of the camp-meeting, and for the conducting of its public and social religious exercises, as in their judgment shall most conduce to carrying forward the work of God in our midst."

Article XI. prescribed the way in which alterations in, or amendments to, the constitution, thus framed, should be made.

The officers of the Association now chosen for the ensuing year were, President, Rev. George M. Carpenter, Presiding Elder of Providence District. Secretary, Hebron Vincent, of Edgartown. Treasurer, Henry Bradley, of Holmes Hole. Agent of the meeting, Sirson P. Coffin, of Edgartown. Finance Committee, Jeremiah Pease, of Edgartown; Henry Bradley, of Holmes Hole; Caleb L. Ellis and A. D. Hatch, of New Bedford; Joshua Remington and Iram Smith, of Fall River; Pardon M. Stone, William A. Wardwell, and William B. Lawton, of Providence; John C. Scott, of Millville;

Cyms Washburn, of East Weymouth; Elisha Harris, of Phœnix; James Davis, of Pawtucket; William Hutchinson, of Taunton; and Lot Phinney, of Osterville.

At one of the meetings of the Association, it was voted that this meeting will fully sustain the Finance Committee in any effort or expense to suppress any and all violations of the Sabbath.

Near the close of the camp-meeting it appeared that the indebtedness of the Association remaining unprovided for was three hundred and five dollars and eighteen cents. Also, at a meeting of the Association at which the above exhibit appeared, a report of the Finance Committee previously made, relating to sundry improvements, having undergone some amendments, was adopted. This report provided for the erection of a new preachers' stand and the reseating of the ground the ensuing year, all to be done on new and improved plans. It also provided for additional means of lighting the ground, and appropriated two hundred and fifty dollars to pay a man for taking care of the fixtures and other property left here during the year, and for work done by him in clearing up the grounds. The report also included an appropriation of five hundred and forty-five dollars to meet current expenses.

In closing this chapter, embodying as it does so many matters of importance, I append another of those friendly outside views. It is in two letters, written upon the ground by the late Colonel Isaac O. Barnes, of Boston, and published in the Boston Courier. We have already had some means of seeing how true a prophet was the writer.

"CAMP MEETING, EDGARTOWN, August 23.

"The public, from year to year, seem to take more and more interest in these religious assemblages, and especially in this one upon the Vineyard Island. Whether it is the insular locality, or the better moral condition of the people, I do not know; but something seems to have rendered this one of the most quiet and orderly religious convocations ever seen or known amongst us.

"There are within a short rifle-shot of where I am writing, at least five thousand people, in their tents, or promenading along the avenues of surrounding trees; and, I venture to say, you cannot find any town in New England, with as many inhabitants, more perfectly quiet.

"This grove is nearly opposite Holmes Hole, although it is within the town of Edgartown. It is on a promontory known to all sailors as 'East Chop,' and directly upon the waters of the Vineyard Sound.

"There are more in number and tonnage of vessels, of all sorts and descriptions, which pass this point, than at any other place in the United States, — except it is Gay Head, at the entrance of the same sound. It is a low estimate to say that they will equal in the aggregate, annually, fifty thousand.

"From this and other points on the island there are the most splendid sea-views in the world. The fine sea-bathing, the endless variety and abundance of fishes, and the bracing and exhilarating atmosphere, all contribute to render this one of the most desirable watering-places, aside from the circumstance of these annual religious assemblages.

"Our people do not know the very great difference in the temperature of the atmosphere between this place and Nahant and Cape Ann. It is always sufficiently cool here, because, let the wind blow from any quarter, it must come over deep sea-water; but when it comes from the east, before reaching this point it is robbed of that cold chill which it always has at Nahant and on the east side of Cape Cod. Very few have reflected how suddenly the atmosphere imparts heat or receives it, when coming in contact with any matter.

" When the breeze comes from the broad ocean — away from the outlet of Baffin's Bay and from the ice-water of Newfoundland, it must be chilly — bad for respiration in weak lungs; but let it but touch for an hour, or for a moment, upon the sands of Cape Cod, and it is tempered and prepared for the most delicate organs. People will find this out soon, and resort here in myriads to build their summer residences. This place is more healthy than Newport, as I will be glad to demonstrate to you from the most authentic tables. These people, who are now so comfortable in their tents around me, — five thousand of them at least, — with steamboat after steamboat arriving almost every hour in the day, loaded with men, women, and children, — these people all know how healthful are the breezes which reach them on East Chop. I could wish, with all my heart, that our Boston citizens would turn their attention once to the very superior advantages of this their own island, instead of resorting to a neighboring state to breathe an atmosphere not as genial, not as healthful, as that of any part of this. Some enterprising men will make princely fortunes here in purchasing the lands, which will soon be in demand, in my judgment.

"If any one of your able corps of newspaper makers can be spared for a day from his duties, — can escape from the heat and dust of the city only for twenty-four hours, — pray let him hie himself hither, and prove what I tell you of the qualities of the air, and partake of the hospitalities of Martha's Vineyard.

"They have the very best fresh water here one ever tastes — plenty of wholesome food, well-cooked and well-served. Arriving on the ground, let any man, woman, or child only inquire for Sirson P. Coffin, Esq., the superintendent of the whole grounds, tents and everything, and my word for it, he or she will find just as good accommodations as can be desired by any reasonable being."

"CAMP GROUND, EDGARTOWN, Aug. 24.

"MY DEAR COURIER: Since writing you yesterday, the people have arrived here in such continual throngs that it is impossible to ascertain the number now on the ground.

"There are accommodations for fifteen thousand, and it is anticipated that as many as that number will have arrived by to-morrow night or

Sunday morning. It is almost impossible to give your readers any adequate idea of the manner of living here. It seems to the inexperienced as if it were impossible to render such an immense number of people comfortable; and yet such is the system, and so perfect the order, upon the grounds, that no one has the least reason to complain of any discomfort.

"There are more than five hundred tents, all told, being at least sixty more than were ever built before. Many of the tents are made of wood, the boards being grooved and tongued, well shingled, made perfectly water-tight, with a ventilator on the top, finished elegantly, even to knobs on the outside doors. The streets and avenues upon which these tents are built are laid out with as much precision and as rectangular as if it had been done by William Penn. The streets and avenues are all named. The preachers' stand is supplied with seats for two thousand five hundred people. The bell is rung at sunrise to call every one from bed; again at eight o'clock, for prayer-meeting in the society-tents; then at ten, two, and seven, for public services at the stand. At ten o'clock at night, all persons not provided with lodgings on the ground retire, and those belonging to the ground go into their tents for the night. There are printed rules for the government of the camp-meeting, and they are carefully and rigidly enforced. Plenty of policemen are here, but they seem to have nothing to do officially.

"The character of the discourses delivered here is of a much higher order than in years past; indeed, many of the speakers are well-educated men, and certainly they are eloquent beyond many men you will hear in the pulpits of other denominations.

"I wish it were possible for you to be with us."

CHAPTER IV.

CAMP-MEETING OF 1861.

WHO can doubt that this camp-meeting is an institution of progress? From the little cleared spot in the dense wood, with its nine rude tents, in 1835, it has been enlarged, from time to time, till now it is a large, circular area, sufficient to accommodate its thousands, having over forty society tents fronting upon it. A new and beautiful stand, devised the year previous, had been erected, contrasting greatly with former ones. It is the same that now graces the place. In its shape it presents five sides of an octagon, with a straight back. It is about twenty feet in length, having a roof projecting six feet each way, all sides being open except the back; and will seat some thirty or forty persons. There is a slightly elevated platform, a few feet in width, along the front; and beyond, a large open space, or altar, enclosed by a railing, within which singers may take their positions, and anxious persons come forward for prayers. The building was neatly painted. With its appendages, it cost about five hundred dollars.

The new seating of the ground, it will be recollected, was also in the design for improvements adopted the preceding year. The plan for this was drawn by Perez Mason, Esq., of Providence, R. I. It was on a grand scale; and the seatings were constructed with backs,—a great convenience,—instead of the plain board seats of former times. There were thus provided fixed accommodations for from three to four thousand people. On the great days of the meetings, which are usually the Sabbaths, ten thousand persons might find convenient positions, either sitting or standing, and listen to the word of life uttered from the stand. The cost of the seating was about one thousand dollars.

But the principal area and circle of tents, although so large, constituted, even at that period, but a small part of the encampment. Avenues, and tents of different descriptions, extended, more or less thickly, over some fifteen or more broad acres.

The entire cost of the preparations that year, including that of the new stand and seating, did not fall much short of the snug sum of two thousand dollars. The Agent of the ground, and the very efficient Finance Committee, had spared no reasonable pains or expense requisite to make the arrangements satisfactory and agreeable. As contemplated the previous year, a laboring man had been retained upon the premises, most of the intervening time, to protect the property left here, in store or otherwise, and also to clear up underbrush, and improve the grounds in the outskirts, as well as to clear off the leaves and other rubbish from the central portions. In addition to the many hundreds of society and family tents and houses, some of which were spacious and costly, there was an increased number of buildings of other descriptions — some where catering was done for the multitude, and some for other useful and sanitary purposes. There were about fifteen licensed boarding tents, with varying capacities for accommodations, seating from fifty to four hundred persons. When the throngs were here, the tables were often replenished and refilled with hungry ones several times at the same meal. There was also a refreshment stand under cover, kept, as for many years, by William Vinson, of Edgartown, a gentleman whose counters were literally loaded with excellent articles of food, in great varieties. Many hundreds, perhaps a thousand persons, might satisfy their wants daily at this tent. Then the washer-women had several tents, and the barbers and boot-blacks had their habitations. Last, but not least, there was a photographer's establishment, where those who wished could be supplied with pictures. These places, however, for supplying the needful and the desirable, were mostly in what were then somewhat retired portions of the encampment.

This camp-meeting was appointed to commence August the 13th. We were expecting large numbers to arrive by the steamers on the day of beginning. The Canonicus was announced to make two trips a day, down from New Bedford, for several successive days. But a very heavy storm prevented the realization of the expectations of men. The severity of this storm exceeded anything of the kind ever before experienced in connection with our meetings on this ground. There was no preaching till the evening of the second day, and then only in two of the larger tents. A powerful wind accompanied the intense rain, laying prostrate quite a number of tents, and injuring others. No one, however, was seriously hurt. The question might well arise, in the minds of some, whether we were not all, in our cotton-top houses, drenched by the rain. Some, no doubt, did suffer inconvenience; but probably most did not. Although it was somewhat chilly, the writer can say, that, for himself, and that part of his little family group with him, they dwelt quite secure here in the wilderness, trusting in their Father, who "rides upon the wings of the wind," and whose paternal care never ceases. The damage done to some of the tents, whose occupants had not arrived, might, very likely, have been prevented, had their owners been here to take care of them.

On account of this very unpropitious weather, which had prevented most of the people from coming to the ground, the Association voted to add two days to the length of this camp-meeting, and fixed the time of closing to be on Thursday evening of the next week, instead of Tuesday evening, provided arrangements to that end could be effected with the steamboat and railroad. Jeremiah Pease, Esq., was appointed a committee to make such arrangements, if practicable.

Whether, owing to the state of the country, now plunged into a terrible war, the meeting would be as largely attended as in the previous two years, was, of course, now rendered still more problematical. But we were hoping that Christians, both of the ministry and laity, would so feel their dependence on the great Giver of all good, in this our time of need, that, in spirituality, at least, the meeting would exceed the meetings held here in previous years.

Three of the large society tents were wrecks, viz., those of Edgartown, Westport, and Chestnut Street, Providence. Other tents had their coverings considerably rent. The eastern part of the camp, near the "Prairie," suffered the most severely. Soon after the Edgartown tent fell, a large tree near it also parted company with its roots; but fortunately it did no harm to life or limb in its fall.

The morning of Thursday, the 15th, gave promise of better things to come. The boats had made one stormy trip the day before, bringing a few ministers and others. The clouds were scattered, and the multitudes were now expected soon. An encouraging spirit prevailed. The repulse caused by the war of elements at the beginning, and the *seeming* defeat, after so extensive preparations, may have dampened the ardor of the timid, and elicited speculation on the part of those not having much sympathy with our gatherings here; but we hoped to profit by the trial, as well as by our errors of the past, and to put ourselves in better condition of mind than before to meet the trained forces of spiritual wickedness, especially the great director of them—"the prince of the power of the air." We trusted that here, as in the country, where the great war of the rebellion had begun to rage, partial defeats at first would prove but the sure precursors of ultimate and lasting victories. In each case we should not be discouraged, but prepare, and trust. The glorious orb of day had begun to shed his cheering beams upon us, infusing joy and gladness all around. Some of the injured tents were being put to rights again. Still other new ones were erected, and all seemed hopeful and prosperous. The public seats were becoming dry, and we were expecting to hear once more the clarion notes of the preacher in the open air, from the stand. The voices of prayer and praise were again heard in the grove.

Our anticipations were realized. There was preaching, that day, by Revs. C. A. Merrill, James Dean, of Lowell, and Dr. Moses L. Scudder, of New York. The first named discoursed upon "Christ's Welcome to the Blessed;" the second, on "Choosing the Better Part, which should not be taken away from its possessor;" and the last named, on the "Choice of Moses, made by Faith, preferring to identify himself with the people of God, rather than be called the son of Pharaoh's daughter." Such was the brilliancy of the day, that it seemed as though the sun was really intent upon making amends for his refusal to shine during the previous two days. The people came in crowds, friend greeted friend, and time again passed joyously.

It is a thought which not unfrequently occurs to those who are familiar with the fact, that members and ministers of the Methodist denomination are probably more extensively acquainted with each other than are those of any other religious people. This, doubtless, in a great measure, is the result of the peculiarities of their church organization, especially those which relate to the itinerant system. By means of the general and annual conferences, the preachers become conversant with vast numbers of their brethren in the ranks, especially those of any considerable prominence, very many of whom they come to know personally; and as a great many of the laity attend these conferences, they are but very little behind their clerical friends in their knowledge of the talents and peculiar traits of these public men, especially as they frequently have occasion to be reconnoitring in view of a supply for their own particular society. The camp-meetings, however, afford the greatest facilities for making and renewing acquaintances with large numbers of the membership of the churches and societies.

These extensive gatherings of Christian people cannot fail to promote and foster the true social element. The facts verify the suggestion; for we are of late years manifesting a tendency at these meetings of allowing our social and sociable qualities to trench quite too much upon the more decidedly spiritual of our religious duties. We have evidently great need of watchfulness on this score, lest the benefits which should be made secondary, be allowed to supersede the original, primary object to be sought here.

On the morrow, Friday, another beautiful morning smiled in upon us. The camp began to exhibit much of its wonted glow of life and animation. The voice of praise, mingling with the notes of the winged songsters, broke upon the stilly morning air, reminding us of those grateful words in a venerated old book, — "the Book of books," — "The winter is over and gone, the flowers appear on the earth, the time of the singing of birds has come, and the voice of the turtle is heard in our land."

The public exercises at the stand to-day were, preaching, in the forenoon, by Rev. N. Bemis, of Sandwich; in the afternoon, by Rev. H. S. White, of Providence; and in the evening, instead of a set sermon, there were addresses by Rev. Messrs. McDonald, of New Bedford, and Livesey, of Newport.

The Rev. N. P. Philbrook, Presiding Elder of the Sandwich District, was Superintendent of this camp-meeting, and President of the Association, and in these responsible positions acquitted himself well. Dr. G. S. Stevens, of Providence, was again chosen Chorister.

The general rules of the meeting were the same, essentially, as for several previous years. They were repeatedly read to the audience, and copies of them were extensively posted, and otherwise distributed, as usual, so that none who should commit a breach of them could plead ignorance in extenuation of the violation. As on other occasions, the hours for public service at the stand, and those of rising in the morning and retiring at night, were indicated by the ringing of the bell.

By a regulation of the Camp-meeting Association, all tents and houses, or cottages, were required to be licensed; for which license a fee was paid to aid in defraying the expenses of preparing and fitting up fixtures upon the ground. Another measure of the Association provided for a strong watch by day and by night. The grove, this year, was finely lighted evenings, by Topham's Patent Whale Oil Burners, wholly at the expense of the owner as to the use of the burners. The ground was never so well lighted before. Near the close of the meeting, the Association passed a vote of thanks to Mr. Topham for the gratuitous use of these brilliant lamps.

Saturday. The numbers arriving were now large. The main entrance to the area was assuming its accustomed appearance of stir and bustle. Broadway was becoming animated, the various lesser avenues lively, and from the head of Trinity Park was one of the most pleasant and picturesque views, within the scope of which teeming thousands moved.

The sermons of this day were by Rev. J. W. Willet, of Chatham, Rev. L. D. Davis, of Warren, R. I., and Rev. D. B. Randall, a veteran preacher from the Maine Conference.

Exercises at the stand, following many of the

sermons, and the prayer-meetings in the large tents, were becoming scenes of much interest.

The Sabbath was, as usual, as to the numbers in attendance, the great day of the meeting. Some six or seven thousand listened to the preaching. There were judged to be in all, in and about the ground, some ten thousand people. The day abounded in efforts for their good. The Love Feast was opened at eight o'clock in the morning by the aged and venerable father, Rev. Daniel Webb, of Barnstable, the oldest effective Methodist minister in the United States. There were fervent praying, laconic speeches, soul-stirring singing, and, above all, the presence of the Holy Spirit. The patriarchal man above named, and the almost equally patriarchal and venerable Rev. Lewis Bates, spoke with much feeling and with great effect of their early lives, and the wonderful things God had wrought for this people since. Both of these men have since gone to their rewards. The sermons of the day were by able men. That of the forenoon was by Rev. Mr. De Hass, of New York, on Rom. xi. 33. In the afternoon the Rev. Mr. Twombly, of

Charlestown, preached from Zeph. ii. 3; and in the evening, Rev. Mr. McDonald, of New Bedford, discoursed on Isa. lv. 6. The sermon of the forenoon was followed by a telling address by Rev. B. W. Gorham, from the State of New York.

In addition to the regular public services at the stand, the few friends styling themselves the "flying artillery," arranged for extra preaching exercises at hours and at places in and about the encampment, and at landings, so as to reach those who otherwise might not hear a sermon or anything of the kind during the day. At the early hour of six o'clock in the morning, an audience listened to a stirring discourse by the Rev. L. B. Bates, son of the venerable Christian warrior before referred to. He showed himself worthy, as his sire before him had done, of being a descendant of the martyr, John Rogers.

The day was bright and fair, and, in religious interest, closed very much as a good day of a camp-meeting used to close twenty years before. There were several conversions during the day, and friends grew very hopeful as to results.

On Monday morning the sacramental service was held, opened by the Rev. Mr. Farrington, of Providence. The sermons of the day were by Revs. J. Howson, B. W. Gorham, and A. N. Bodfish. Thousands who came only for the Sabbath had left, but many others came.

At meetings of the Association, held at different times during the camp-meeting, the various items of business were attended to. All the old officers, not before named, were reëlected, and nearly all the old members of the Finance Committee. Reports were submitted and acted upon, the state of the finances found to be healthy, and the appropriations for another year, amounting to eight hundred and ninety dollars, promptly made. The following vote will show what was the pay of the Agent of the meeting at that time.

"Voted, unanimously, that the thanks of the Association be given to brother Coffin for his valuable services, and that he be paid the sum of fifty dollars to remunerate him in some measure for his services."

Tuesday. Friend Tillinghast was here again this morning with the children. The weather was unexpectedly delightful. Our ranks were growing thin. As was foreseen by some, the lengthening of the time on account of the heavy weather at the first, which was done without the knowledge of those coming from a distance, could not have been provided for in their preparations, and those who had already arrived before the storm could not, of course, have made provision for such a change. At most, one day was all that should have been added. Still the floating population that came on daily was somewhat of a counterpoise for the many who were obliged to leave.

The preaching on that day was by Rev. John B. Gould, of Providence, in the forenoon, Rev. David H. Ela, of Bristol, R. I., in the afternoon, and Rev. Richard Donkersley, of Cumberland, R. I., in the evening. The sermon of the afternoon was followed by exhortations, and by prayers for anxious persons, long continued. Some professed conversion ere the exercise closed.

The king of day was pouring in upon us this morning his mellow beams, and all nature around was smiling; but the noise and stir attendant upon a partial evacuation of the camp struck the ear unpleasantly. To be sure, we could not think it strange that those who came early were leaving at the time first allotted, nor could we deny that almost every one had the privilege of coming and going when he pleased; and we, who were under obligation to stay, must bear it as best we might. Even the worthy president of the meeting had to leave in order to meet an engagement elsewhere, his vacated chair being filled by Rev. Charles H. Titus, formerly a Presiding Elder. Thus we sometimes changed commanders here, as well as in the army of the country. It was pretty hard, however, for any officer, skilful as he might be, to organize our army here into anything more than volunteer regiments, and that for only a short time. Brigades are scarcely formed before we begin to change positions. Our greatest success is by "companies." These hold together the best, and, with their chosen captains, enlist, to a great extent, for the war. But whatever others might do, either the officers or the rank and file, to the ever-busy secretary of the camp there was no discharge. He must stay to write up till the last word is said. He, however, at this time, was cherishing the hope of receiving at least a furlough in a day or two.

On Wednesday the sermons were by Revs. S. F. Upham, William Livesey, and Edward A. Lyon. Although this was not the day fixed by supplementary law for the closing scene, many, on their part, took the matter into their own hands. It was not exactly a stampede, yet a very large part of those remaining from the previous day changed the place of their bivouac. Enough were left, probably, to take care of the sick and wounded. As the enemy had been somewhat repulsed, and seemed not likely to attack our lines again in force, we felt very safe with our comparatively small numbers.

Literally, the spirit of true patriotism seemed to manifest itself quite frequently during the exercises of this camp-meeting. At one o'clock, a meeting was held at the stand to pray for our beloved country. It was well attended. Earnest supplications were offered up, and several short and appropriate addresses were made.

At the close, the following resolution, offered by Rev. J. A. Dean, of East Greenwich, and seconded by Rev. J. H. Twombly, of Charlestown, was adopted, without debate, by a rising vote: "Resolved, That we, who are in attendance at the Martha's Vineyard Camp-meeting, respectfully request the officers of our national government, and of our armies, to maintain, as far as possible, the sanctity of the Sabbath; so that neither in camp nor field, nor in the transportation of troops, there be any secular duties required on that day that are not absolutely necessary."

On Thursday morning, at eight o'clock, we were called together at the stand to hear the parting address. It was given by Rev. B. W. Gorham. We were then dismissed with the doxology and the benediction.

About seventy ministers of our own denomination, and some of other churches, had been present more or less of the time. Our visiting brethren from other conferences did us excellent service, and some of them, who had never been with us before, were agreeably disappointed in the amount of spirituality manifested, and indeed there was a good degree. Preachers and members seemed to feel that there was a loud call for extra exertion, and many entered into labor in good earnest. The preaching was in the spirit, and the praying, and singing, and exhorting were with faith and fervor. On several of the later days of the meeting, the exercises at the stand, following the preaching, were powerful and long-continued, not closing on the last evening till the hour of ten. Many of the tent-meetings were also seasons to be remembered. About thirty persons were converted, the brethren much quickened, and the glory of other years seemed to be returning.

It was stated that, from various unusual causes, those who liberally furnished tables for us in the wilderness made a losing business of it. However this may have been, very many in attendance at the meeting proved the verity of the divine word — that they who trust in God "shall verily be fed," *spiritually*.

CHAPTER V.

CAMP-MEETING OF 1862.

LIKE the ancient Israelites, who maintained through successive centuries their great periodical feasts, most religious denominations have statedly their particular gatherings of the people, or their representatives, such as associations, conventions, conferences, and the like. In addition to the ordinary occasions of the last-named description, the Methodists, although not the first to inaugurate them, have long been accustomed to hold, annually, for extra religious efforts, grove, or camp, meetings. The twenty-seventh of a series of such meetings was about to be commenced — nay, it had, in a manner, commenced some days before the time appointed. Quite a number of both ministers and people having convened, some three hundred persons met together for worship on a preceding Sabbath. Rev. C. H. Titus and Rev. John B. Gould were the preachers of the day.

In the earlier days of camp-meetings, a small site a few rods in breadth, was cleared of underbrush by friends in the vicinity, and the companies from the various neighboring societies did not repair thither till the day assigned for the beginning. When arrived upon the spot, they at once erected their tents — which were not always the most symmetrical, — many of them having frames rudely constructed at the time, and covered with old sails, or such other material as could be obtained for the purpose. Now, in this permanent place of resort, the many hundreds of tent frames, together with cottages and other buildings, remained, of course, through the year; and, by an arrangement with some one living in the vicinity, the tent covers were stored and cared for, and then readjusted to the frame some days before they were needed for occupancy. This secured a dry tent floor, or ground, good weather being seized upon for the purpose. On Friday of the week preceding that of the meeting, nearly all the large tents, and many of the small ones, were covered. On the day preceding that of the commencement, nearly every part of the encampment was in its beautiful dress. The large tents prostrated by the gale the year previous, had, of course, to be "reconstructed." On rebuilding that belonging to the Edgartown church, our thoughts very naturally reverted to the past, and the writer cannot let slip unimproved, in this place, the opportunity of paying a brief tribute to the memory of him who had been, for many years, the "tent-master," or "superintendent" of this tent, but who, a week or two before, ascended to "the house not made with hands, eternal in the heavens." In person he would meet with us here no more, although his sainted spirit might often mingle with us, unseen, in our prayers and praises. He was one of the few who first agreed to the selection of this site, and was one of the first lessees. He had ever been a firm supporter of the meetings, having in his high official position rendered invaluable service in the preservation of order. Dying at an advanced age, he had long been a highly esteemed and valuable citizen. Such was Isaiah D. Pease, Esq., of Edgartown, for thirty-nine years a member of the Methodist Episcopal church, and for more than forty years sheriff of Dukes County.

At this camp-meeting, commencing August 5, the Rev. George M. Carpenter, Presiding Elder of the Providence District, was chosen to preside, and was again, for the year, President of the Association. Hon. William B. Lawton was chosen Chorister. Some changes were initiated with regard to the religious exercises. One of them was, that instead of holding prayer-meetings in all the society tents at the same time, several tents' companies were to unite in one meeting, so that there should be but three or four such meetings at any given hour. It was thought that such union-meetings would better concentrate the effective forces of the encampment. The measure may have been a good one for the first day or two, but was of doubtful utility as the numbers increased in the further stages of the camp-meeting.

The first public service was, as usual, on the evening of the day appointed to commence. On the following day, in the forenoon, the sermon was by Rev. Samuel C. Brown, of East Weymouth, on Zach. xiv. 6, 7. The part dwelt upon was, "At evening time it shall be light."

At the conclusion of the sermon, the Rev. Dr. Sears, President of Brown University, delivered an address of about a half hour's length, following up and further illustrating the doctrine advanced by the previous speaker, in strains of rare eloquence and power. It was an address which, while it showed the highly-cultivated intellect and the beautiful style of a master, portrayed also the incomparable excellency of Christianity, especially in its power to render the evening of the believer's life the scene of holy triumph rather than one of gloom and sadness, as it often is to the unregenerate.

Rev. N. Bemis, of New Bedford Fourth Street Church, preached in the afternoon, followed by Camp-meeting John Allen, in an energetic and characteristic exhortation.

The sermon of the evening was by Rev. E. A. Lyon, of Fairhaven. Rev. C. H. Payne, of Fall River, gave a spirited address.

It had been rumored that a war-meeting was to be held some time during the encampment; but no such meeting had been determined upon.

We were, however, pleased to learn, that our excellent governor, John A. Andrew, intended to visit the ground some time during the meeting. As governor of the commonwealth, he had done much to aid in putting down the existing rebellion, and we were quite sure he could visit no more loyal people than those assembled in this hallowed grove.

Among the distinguished laymen visiting the place this day was the Hon. Jacob Sleeper, of Boston.

Our ever-vigilant police made a descent upon some fifteen or more gallons of alcoholic liquors, secreted in the woods. The "contraband" article was brought into the store-room, and put in "safe keeping." It would hardly be needed for work in the trenches. It would, of course, be "confiscated" and "freed."

The sermons of Thursday were by Rev. William Studley, of New Bedford County Street Church, on "The Faithful Saying;" Rev. E. H. Hatfield, of Taunton, on "The Offerings of Cain and Abel;" and Rev. Mr. Thurston, of the New Hampshire Conference, on the "New Birth." The prayer-meeting following the evening sermon was protracted and animated. A pure air, well-furnished tables, and the greetings of friends were among the inspirations of the place; but to the truly devout mind the increased spirit of devotion could not be lost sight of.

On Friday morning we were favored with a refreshing rain, always acceptable in a dry time. The preaching was in tents, by Revs. John Allen, of Maine, B. W. Gorham, of Wyoming Conference, Charles H. Payne, of Fall River, and D. H. Ela, of Woonsocket, R. I.

At two o'clock the stand was occupied by Rev. Mr. Jones, of Worcester, Superintendent of Public Schools. Text, Ps. xxxvi. 18. Theme, "The Richness of God, and the Richness of the Saints *in* God."

The rain in the morning had been succeeded by sunshine, but still, clouds were lowering much of the day. The sky was finally clear; but near evening the dwellers in our city were taken by surprise by one of the heaviest thunderstorms of the season. It being a time of day when our campers enjoy, if disposed, a walk in the neighboring fields, and to the cliffs, not a few were caught in the rain, and came back "skedaddling" to their tents in great confusion.

The evening preaching was in tents again, by Revs. John Allen, N. P. Philbrook, William H. Richards, and William T. Worth.

Although the number gathered here was now quite large, it was evident that from some localities, in other years well represented, the delegations were greatly diminished. The war and the times might account for this. The lack thus occasioned was partly made up by the attendance of some who had usually gone to Eastham, — the camp-meeting at that place having been discontinued, and no other site having yet been substituted for it, — and partly by the presence of considerable delegations from other sections, whose meetings did not occur that week. The Hamilton meeting being appointed for the following week, we had present more or less members from nearly or quite every Methodist church in the city of Boston. The central part of the state was also represented. From Worcester and vicinity there were more than two hundred persons tenting with us.

About the accustomed number of new comers arrived on this day.

At about eleven o'clock that night we had a second part of the thunder-storm, which, in intensity, far exceeded the first. The almost constant lightning's glare, the continued roar of heaven's artillery, and the rain falling almost in torrents, rendered the scene awfully sublime. But it was the voice and work of our Father. We rested securely in our tents, and the following morning "the glorious orb of day" was mildly beaming in upon us.

Saturday. As the more fierce the strife of the battle-field, the larger the scale on which the battle is fought, the more it embodies the strength of the contending belligerents, and the more decisive the triumph of the victors, the more permanent will be the victory and the peace which will follow, — so, in respect to the war of the elements of nature, the fiercer the storm and the tempest, the greater, consequently, will be the purity and serenity of the atmosphere, and the more brilliant the golden beams of the world's luminary. Thus it was the day after the passing by of the tremendous rush to arms of the warring forces above us the previous night. The air was now salubrious, indeed, and the music of voices, the rustling of the foliage, and the notes of the feathered warblers, mingling together, and all borne upon the gentle breezes, made melody, indeed, to the great "Giver of every good and perfect gift." Tranquillity reigned.

The sermons of this day were by Rev. Messrs. J. W. Dadmun, of Worcester, William McDonald, of New Bedford, and B. W. Gorham, of the Wyoming Conference.

One of the attractions of the place at one o'clock to-day was a meeting in one of the large tents, designed especially for the young people of our churches.

It was, indeed, a delightful thing to see some hundreds of beaming, youthful countenances, male and female, devoutly engaged in the service of God together — to hear these young persons pray so ardently, speak so pathetically, and sing so sweetly. The young are no less the hope of the church than of the country.

We hear of casualties by the lightning and by the storm. One aged man living on Edgartown Plain, being feeble, and hurrying from his field to avoid the rain, was so exhausted by the effort that he expired soon after reaching his house. The sloop Bride, of Falmouth, was capsized when within a mile or two of that place, and sunk. There were seven persons on board, all saved by another vessel.

As anticipated, His Excellency Governor Andrew arrived on the ground between the hours of four and five P. M. of this day, accompanied by three members of the Council — Hon. Oakes Ames, G. W. Cochrane, and E. C. Sherman; Colonel J. M. Witherell, of the Governor's Staff, Colonel A. G. Browne, Private Secretary, Hon. Oliver Warner, Secretary of State, A. L. Fernald, Secretary's Deputy, J. P. Clarke, Auditing Deputy, J. B. Spear, Governor's Messenger, and Judge Thomas Russell, of Boston. On the arrival of the Governor and suite near the office and storage building, there being no public service in progress at the time, he was received by a large company of people with patriotic cheers. His Excellency responded in some appropriate remarks, stating the object of his visit — his desire to enjoy a day or two of quiet here.

By invitation of the President of the meeting, the Governor took a seat on the stand during the evening sermon, withdrawing at its close. He took lodgings at the residence of Hon. Benjamin Davis, near the encampment.

Sabbath. An extra service was held at the stand at the very early hour of six o'clock, when there was a sermon by Rev. Joseph Marsh, of Orleans, on "the threefold cord, which cannot easily be broken." At eight o'clock was the Love Feast, conducted by Rev. Thomas Ely, of North Bridgewater. It was attended by some thousands. Among those who gave testimony were the venerable Daniel Webb, several times referred to elsewhere, the Hon. M. F. Odell, M. C. from Brooklyn, N. Y., and five members of the New York "Praying Band," or "Flying Artillery." These last were all remarkable laymen, and were making a good impression, adding interest to the meeting.

Rev. John Lindsey, of New York, late a professor in Wesleyan University, preached an eloquent sermon at ten o'clock, from Luke xii. 15. The "Praying Band" then, by request, took charge of the service, and continued it as a prayer meeting with great earnestness till about one o'clock. Crowds came on the boats during the forenoon, the Island Home alone bringing from Nantucket and the Cape one thousand persons. About ten thousand were in the Grove, some six thousand to eight thousand of whom were within hearing in the afternoon.

Rev. J. A. M. Chapman, of Fall River, preached the sermon at two o'clock. Text, Psalm xv. 1. Governor Andrew, who, with Hon. J. H. W. Page, of Boston, was seated on the stand, being previously invited to make an address to the people at this time, did so with great effect. He occupied about an hour and a quarter. The place, the occasion, and the day, were very appropriately recognized as suggesting the taking of a Christian view, although His Excellency confessed he had no license to preach. Such a view he took of the present state of the country, and the history of our liberties. He spoke of the cause of our troubles, Slavery, which he believed it was God's design to destroy before giving us peace, and urged it as a religious duty to hasten to the rescue. These ministers of the gospel were here laboring to enlist volunteers for the Son of God. He was here the head enlisting officer for the war, and did not think it wrong for men to enlist in this cause on the Sabbath. He urged the duty, and hoped the Old Bay State would never have a man raised by conscription. The address was received with great favor, and, instead of the usual demonstrations of applause, which it was desired should not, for reasons, be made, but which it was hard to repress, the Chief Magistrate was repeatedly greeted with true Methodistic shouts and "Amens," which he seemed very much to appreciate and relish. As a whole it was a grand good meeting, and calculated to promote "the truth," which the Governor sought to do. We said on the occasion, "Health and long life to our good Executive." But, alas! he has since, very suddenly, gone to the world of spirits.

The sermon of the evening was by Rev. Charles H. Payne, of Fall River, on "Hostility to God." Text, Isaiah xlv. 9. The "Praying Band" followed the preaching in a meeting conducted in their own peculiar way, which proved to be successful, resulting in the conversion of several individuals. It was not unlike scenes of former years, and continued till ten o'clock. These laymen were really ahead of most of the ministers in the manner of their revival labors.

This Sabbath was a memorable day. Besides the notable men already named as having been present, I should mention Judges Day and Marston, of Barnstable, and Gardner, of Nantucket, Collector Goodrich, of Boston, Collector Swift, of Yarmouth, and Hon. John Morissey, Sergeant at Arms. The weather was magnificent. The Governor and suite left late in the afternoon.

Under the direction of a Committee on extra services, there was preaching at several outposts. At six o'clock P. M., there was preaching by Rev. Lewis B. Bates, near the Cliffs, at what was called the "Juniper Tree." About a thousand people were collected to hear. At the same hour, Christeller, a Jew, who was converted on this ground some years previous, preached near the main entrance to the Circle. About the same time there was a large gathering in Trinity Park, where swelled, in grand chorus, the music of voices. These several assemblages occurring purposely at an hour when the regular public services were not in session, large numbers flocked to the several locations named.

Monday. The sacramental service was held this morning, conducted by Rev. James D. Butler of the Seamen's Bethel, New Bedford. In the forenoon, Rev. David H. Ela preached on "Being reconciled to God." In the afternoon, Rev. John Livesey, of Allen Street Church, discoursed on "The Benefits of Youthful Piety." The sermon of the evening was by Rev. J. W. Willet, on "Reasons for listening to the Word of the Lord."

Tuesday. Although our numbers were greatly diminished, the regular religious services were continued. Rev. James D. Butler preached from Acts ii. 41. Rev. William V. Morrison, then of Sandwich, took for his text Mark ix. 23: "Jesus said unto him, if thou canst believe, all things are possible to him that believeth." The evening sermon, which was the last, was by Rev. John B. Gould, on "Well Doing." He was followed in earnest addresses by several others, after which, and singing the doxology, the congregation was dismissed with the benediction by Rev. Mr. Carpenter, the President of the meeting.

During this camp-meeting we had had the usual excellent police regulations, and order had been maintained. Great efforts had been made to preserve the integrity of the place against the intrusions of evil doers. In addition to the lot of liquor previously named, found in the woods, several parcels had been discovered in secluded places, or detected in vessels by the shores. The taking of these fire-waters into possession had, doubtless, saved us the trouble of their crazing effects upon some who were their ready patrons. Other forms of evil, too, had been greatly averted.

As a whole, this had been a very interesting camp-meeting. About thirty persons had professed conversion, and the general religious feeling was deep and abiding.

One of the special features of interest this year was the appearance of the "Camp-meeting Herald," which attracted much attention by its spicy and interesting articles, and sold rapidly. It is believed to be the first journal of the kind ever printed.

The plan of licensing tents and cottages for a fee was somewhat improved upon this year, and was found to work well.

During the encampment there were held several meetings of the Association, as at other times. At these meetings the business interests had been cared for. It was voted at one of them, not to employ any steamboat for the conveyance of passengers and baggage to and from the camp-meeting next year, the agent of which will not agree not to run to and from the ground on the Sabbath; and that, in case no such boat can be had, the meeting be not held over the Sabbath.

At its closing session for this occasion, it appeared, from a report submitted by the Finance Committee, that all the expenses of the current year, — some eight hundred dollars, — would be met at once, besides paying a considerable part of the existing debt incurred in the building of the new stand, and the reseating of the ground, a year or two previous. The Committee were authorized to make all needful arrangements for another year, under an appropriation not exceeding eight hundred dollars. Instead of choosing any one man " Agent," the Finance Committee were made the " Agent " for the ensuing year. Some important alterations were made in the Constitution of the Association, one of which extended membership to certain persons not before included, and another related to the time of making the annual reports of the Agent and Treasurer, and the manner of disposing of the same. At one of the sessions a letter was read by Rev. Charles H. Payne, of Fall River, received from a minister of another Conference, on the subject of increasing the usefulness of camp-meetings, and the best means to be adopted to that end. The subject being an important one, and there not being convenient time then for sufficient deliberation, a Committee was appointed, of which Mr. Payne was the Chairman, to consider the matter, and report at the camp-meeting the following year.

This is a mixed world. All is not smooth, all is not sunshine.

> " Each pleasure hath its poison, too,
> And every sweet a snare."

Joy and sorrow are often mingled in the same

cup. One might well suppose that after the enjoyments of a delightful week in the umbrageous grove, in the midst of friends and of friendly associations, and participating in the religious spirit of the occasion, we would, at the end of such sojourn, nevertheless, rejoice as well, without alloy, to have the privilege of returning to our homes, where are our friends, our business, and "safe abode." But the closing up of a camp-meeting is, after all, attended with feelings of sadness, more or less. We are leaving a place of hallowed memories. Perhaps those of our family circle who have been tenting here with us have gone already, and left us deserted, to spend a lonely night. Then, the masses of the people having already left the ground, the comparatively few are packing up, striking tents, and the like. This process may have been going on for a day or two, in some parts of the camp, inasmuch as some leave, as well as come to the place, sooner than others. But still we must leave; and, should we never greet each other here again, we hope to meet where parting shall be no more forever.

CHAPTER VI.

CAMP-MEETING OF 1863.

THE heated term had been long and quite oppressive even to us, who are favored and fanned by the refreshing sea-breezes. How grateful, then, to those who are literally hemmed in by stone and brick walls, in the cities full, to be able to leave their sweltering abodes, and hie them away to the shady grove on this sea-girt isle!

The world — at least that portion of it called Southern Massachusetts — was astir. Hot weather and camp-meetings united — the one by the power of propulsion, and the other by that of attraction — were moving the masses. While Newport, R. I., was having its thousands of visitors, Edgartown was full to repletion, so far as its hotel accommodations were concerned; and if it had possessed but the needed provisions of this sort, it would soon have become the Newport of Massachusetts. But what was wanting in this respect, Wesleyan Grove seemed destined to supply, although in a somewhat different manner.

Camp-meeting had become a great institution in this country; and here, in our favored New England, at least, even the turmoils of war did not seem to interfere with attendance upon its privileges. But this island oasis had become something more than a resort for a week. Hither visitors — most of them regular attendants — had been wending their way, as usual, for several weeks previous to the beginning of the meeting, Christian people had been enjoying a kind of prelude to the camp-meeting proper, and on the Sabbath next preceding it, most of the five hundred people on the ground listened to preaching. Rev. L. D. Davis, of Newport, and Rev. S. C. Brown, of Fall River, were the preachers.

The tents here, this year, were in undiminished numbers, as a whole. A camp-meeting site having been fixed upon and prepared in Yarmouth, instead of the one at Eastham, some of the society tents, long located here, had been removed to that ground, as being more convenient for their occupants to attend. But the tents thus removed were but little missed from the circle, such was its crowded condition. The spacious Chestnut Street Church tent had a new frame, and was in a new position. Several new cottages and tents had been erected. These, and other results of individual and society enterprise, were outside of the general arrangements made by the Finance Committee through the Agent of the meeting, which were ample for the accommodation of all.

One of the greatest advantages of this location, as a camp-meeting site, is its convenient proximity to the waters of the ocean. A delightful walk of less than half a mile, partly through the grove, on a good road, and partly through the open field, brings the multitude of promenaders, who throng the ways, to the rising grounds, or bluffs, by the shore. The prospect here is fine, the air exhilarating; and those who, morning and evening, tried the sea-bath, which many did, acquired a relish for sea-bathing, which was very likely to induce them frequently to repeat the same.

The greatest defect in this grove, then and since, has been, that some of those ancient oaks in the principal area have been losing their crowning foliage. This loss it has been attempted to repair by the setting out of young trees in the more exposed places. The experiment, however, thus far, is not regarded as having been very successful.

This camp-meeting commenced Tuesday, August 18. As elsewhere indicated, our friends, who had been here rusticating the previous week or two, had not been inattentive to religious duties. Prayer-meetings had been held several successive evenings. On Monday evening, the spacious new Matthewson Street tent was crowded, and the exercises were spirited and profitable.

The heavy rain of the previous Sunday night was a great blessing to the camp-meeting, as well as to the public. The roads were made better, and the air became cool, and even autumn-like. The grove was inviting, and the people were coming.

The opening exercise of the camp-meeting proper took place on Tuesday evening. The sermon was by the Rev. Paul Townsend, Presiding Elder of the Providence District, and Superintendent of the meeting. The text was Matt. v. 14: "Ye are the light of the world." It was an able discourse, well adapted to the commencement of our meeting, upon the theme so apparent in the text. Earnest addresses followed from Revs. C. H. Titus, W. Farrington, and S. W. Coggeshall, D. D.

On Wednesday morning the usual prayer-meetings were held in the large tents, or in some of them, at least; and Rev. Charles H. Titus preached, at the usual morning hour, from Mark ix. 24, on the power and practical benefits of Faith. Rev. Charles Morse followed in a telling address, extending remarks on the theme of the sermon.

In the afternoon, Rev. Richard Donkersley, of Baltic, Conn., preached. His theme, which was extensively illustrated, was, "Prayer and labor combined are the efficient instrumentality for the salvation of man." The sermon was followed by an energetic address of some length from Rev. Israel Washburn, late Chaplain of the Massachusetts Twelfth Regiment of Volunteers. He had practised combining prayer and effort. He had given his prayers and his money, and finally had given *himself*, to the country. Mr. W. dwelt somewhat on his experience in the war, so that the service became very much of a war meeting. The good man has since gone to his rest in heaven, where there is no war. The high wind of this afternoon made out-of-doors preaching rather a laborious business; but men in earnest succeeded in making the people hear.

Although there was no uncommon indication of disorder, but otherwise, the crowds coming on — very many of them strangers here — appearing perfectly gentlemanly and lady-like, still the accustomed attention was paid to the publishing and distributing of the rules of the meeting, so that none need commit even the sin of ignorance.

Although good order had been a marked characteristic of the meetings gathering here from year to year, in the present mixed state of society, law and its executors are everywhere found to be needful to prevent and restrain wrong doing, if not for the punishment of evil doers. Were it not for courts and prisons, there would be incomparably more of crime than there is now. So the wholesome rules and efficient police at our camp-meetings contribute to secure the decorum manifest. The day police was organized under Robert C. Topham, Esq., of New Bedford, as its chief; and the night police under the charge of John C. Scott, Esq., of Millville.

The grounds were lighted this year by new street lamps. Cost of lighting, one hundred and six dollars. The tables of the boarding establishments were, as usual, loaded with good things for the inner man. Special Post Office arrangements, as for several years, were made by Sylvanus L. Pease, Esq., former Postmaster at Edgartown.

The sermon of Wednesday evening was by Rev. Charles Morse. Text, John xiii. 26.

The sermons of Thursday were by Rev. S. W. Coggeshall, D. D., of North Rehoboth, Rev. L. R. Thayer, D. D., of Cambridge, and Rev. L. B. Bates, of North Easton.

The preaching on Friday was by Rev. William Livesey, of Fairhaven, Rev. J. H. Twombly, of Charlestown, and Rev. A. J. Church, of

Lawrence. The text of the last named, who was a stranger among us then, was 1 Pet. i. 10: "The sufferings of Christ, and the glory that should follow." The sermon was one of the best ever delivered here.

It being reported that Bishop Simpson was to dedicate a church in Newtonville, about this time, measures were adopted to secure, if possible, the services of that eminent man to preach here on the camp-meeting Sabbath. The endeavor was without success.

On Saturday, a shower prevented preaching at the stand in the forenoon. Revs. John Allen, of Maine, N. P. Selee, of East Harwich, and J. D. King, of Pawtucket, preached in tents. Rev. David H. Ela, of Woonsocket, preached at the stand in the afternoon, and Rev. L. D. Davis, of Newport, in the evening. The theme of the last named was, "The divine existence of God as the Ruler and Governor of men."

Crowds of people came on the boat to-day. Passing around the grounds, near night, great numbers of new faces presented themselves. People came of different denominations, and of no denomination; and so long as they were decorous, as were almost all who came, we heartily welcomed them, and were happy to have them mingle with us in our social circles, and in our religious devotions.

Sabbath. We were somewhat interrupted by thunder showers. The Love Feast, which usually occurs in the morning, was finally held, largely attended, at six o'clock P. M. The forenoon sermon was by Rev. Edward H. Hatfield, of the Fourth Street New Bedford Church, on "The Goodness of God." Rev. Sidney Dean, of Warren, R. I., was the preacher in the afternoon, from Matt. iii. 12 : "Whose fan is in his hand, and he will thoroughly purge his floor." Theme, Christ as an Agitator. It is but even justice to say, that the sermon was one of the best. The Rev. F. S. De Hass, of Brooklyn, N. Y., lately of Memorial Church notoriety, preached in the evening. He treated upon what constitutes the foundation of the Christian church. The congregations of the day were very large.

The sermons on Monday were by Rev. John Allen, of Maine, and Rev. Mr. Bonham, Baptist minister, of Woonsocket, R. I. The tide of humanity set out from the place to-day about as fast as it set in during the last days of the previous week. The closing public service was held at the stand in the evening. Appropriate addresses were delivered by our excellent presiding officer, Rev. Paul Townsend, and several others. The official supervision of the grounds ceased on the following morning.

Many distinguished strangers had been upon the ground during this camp-meeting, including some of the officers of the Nautical School Ship, which anchored in Holmes Hole harbor during the meeting, and remained several days; among them, the accomplished teacher of the boys, Mr. Eldridge, now captain of the ship; also Hon. Thomas D. Eliot, and Rev. Mr. Girdwood, of New Bedford, and Rev. J. T. Robert, LL. D., of Iowa. The numbers of people attending this year were very large. There were never more, except in 1860, the year preceding the war. It was estimated there were ten thousand on the ground on the Sabbath.

There were a few conversions; and the general sentiment was, that the meeting had been a profitable one.

S. P. Coffin, Esq., was chosen Agent; Jeremiah Pease, Esq., Treasurer; and all the old Finance Committee were re-chosen.

It appeared, by the report of the Finance Committee, that the entire expense of the ground, this year, was eight hundred and eighty-nine dollars.

It will be remembered that, up to the time of this camp-meeting, the ownership of these grounds had been in other hands. We had always occupied them under leases from the owners. The subject of purchasing them had of late been agitated. In one of the business meetings, some correspondence upon the subject between the Agent of the meeting and the owner was read, as a part of the report of the Committee upon the subject. The report was laid upon the table for the present, and does not appear to have been called up again during this camp-meeting. Still the Finance Committee and Agent were looking into the feasibility of the project during the year following, in view of a probable purchase in the future.

At one or two of the business meetings the subject of conveyance to the ground, under the vote of the preceding year, was much discussed. It will be recollected that it was then ordered, that, unless a steamer could be secured whose agent would agree not to run on the Sabbath, the camp-meeting this year should be so appointed as not to hold over the Sabbath. But the meeting *had* been appointed to hold over the Sabbath, and yet a boat had been secured whose agent was not pledged as above indicated. The explanations made, however, by the Committee on Transportation, were satisfactory, and the appointment of the meeting, as stated, justified. The Sunday question, with reference to the meeting of next year, was much discussed.

The following votes were passed: —

"That the occupants of every tent, upon retiring for the night, place, or cause to be placed, a pail of water at or near the front or rear entrance to their tent, so that the same may be easy of access in case of fire." Also, —

"That the meeting next year be held from Tuesday evening to the following Tuesday morning; and that the Finance Committee be instructed to employ a boat that will not run on the Sabbath."

CHAPTER VII.

CAMP-MEETING OF 1864.

THE arrangements for the annual camp-meeting in Wesleyan Grove this year were on a grand scale. South of the old encampment, and adjacent thereto, there had been cleared up and laid out, with skill and care, some acres of grove, sufficient to accommodate hundreds of tents and cottages. It was all "lotted," and the lots were numbered. Many of these lots had already been taken up, and some beautiful tents and cottages erected. With a large central circular area, and several avenues parallel to each other, crossed by other avenues or streets, in amphitheatrical order, this new section was of itself sufficiently large for an ordinary camp-meeting. This entire encampment now covered about twenty-six acres. A large number of new and fine cottages had been erected recently,—costing from one hundred and fifty to six hundred dollars,—and many new tents, and the grounds much improved generally. These cottages, like the smaller tents, some of them costly and beautiful, were for the occupancy of families.

Many persons were spending their August vacation from business here. And where, on the coast of New England, could they spend it better—with greater profit to the physical or mental man—than among these grand old oaks, fanned by the refreshing sea-breezes? Some had already spent several weeks here. It was estimated, late in the week preceding the meeting, that there were a thousand people here—as many as the entire number attending some of the earlier camp-meetings in this grove. Nor did those who thus came beforehand for physical and mental invigoration forget their religious obligations. Prayer-meetings were held in some one or more of the large tents every evening. Several ministers had been among the number of sojourners, and public services were held at the stand on the previous Sabbath. Rev. Mark Trafton, of New Bedford County Street Church, and Rev. William McDonald, of Providence Chestnut Street Church, were the preachers.

In the absence of the steamer Monohansett, which had been chartered by the government, the Nantucket boat, the Island Home, was engaged to transport passengers and freight. Arrangements had been made, as on other occasions, for a daily mail to and from the encampment. The crowds came; and, although the prices of board were in advance of those of preceding years, the prospects were in favor of the usual attendance.

The day of beginning, August 16, was fine. Many of the newly-arrived were adjusting the fixtures of their temporary abodes, and things assumed very much the appearance of "a place inhabited." Some, who left here a year or two previous for a new place, came back again this year, concluding, doubtless, that "the old is better." I have alluded to the erection of new cottages. There were now, in all, about forty of these. Of cottages and tents of all kinds, there were now about five hundred, and still lots were selected and engaged to build upon the following year.

On the evening of this day, the first public service of the camp-meeting proper was held at the stand, addressed by Rev. Paul Townsend, Presiding Elder of the Providence District, and President of the meeting, Rev. William T. Harlow, Principal of the Rock River Conference Seminary, and others. These speakers were hopeful of good results. The conviction seemed to be deepening that, while the facilities for physical recuperation and social enjoyment were unsurpassed by any similar place, the great tendency was to overlook the original design of such gatherings — the promotion of spiritual interests; and the great aim of the speakers seemed to be to awaken an increased interest in this greater and higher object.

The preaching on Wednesday was in the forenoon, at the stand, by Rev. Samuel C. Brown; in the afternoon, in large tents, by Rev. Messrs. Willet, Bates, and Gurney; and in the evening, by Rev. Dr. Upham and Rev. C. Noble. The rain continued.

On Thursday, Rev. William T. Harlow, before named, preached on "Grace to help in time of need." The weather in the afternoon required in-doors preaching, and Revs. S. W. Coggeshall, Seth Reed, William V. Morrison, and Rev. Mr. Cone, from the West, were the speakers. The sermon of the evening was by Rev. J. D. King, of Taunton. The prayer-meeting which followed was continued till the hour of ten.

Friday was indeed a day of good things. The sun shone brightly, yet the air was sufficiently cool to be invigorating. The grove was beautiful, light and shade happily blending. The congregations were somewhat increased, and the spirit of the meeting indicated progress. It is true that other things were attended to besides religious worship by many gathered here; for it cannot be denied that very many came, as on other occasions, for purposes of pleasure and recreation, rather than for any higher object,—judging them "by their works." Promenading was followed no less than in former years, and sea-bathing was more extensively practised than ever before. Well as these things are in their places, they should not engross too much of precious time. Nor were they allowed to do so by all. Let illiberal critics say what they will of the decrease of spirituality in the meetings held here, it is averred that hundreds and thousands of Christians, ministers and laymen, came for the same holy purposes and in the same devout spirit as in by-gone days. It does not follow that because we do not live all together in the large tents, and sleep in the straw, that therefore our religion has died out. Having somewhat more of conveniences for the comfort of our bodies may not render our gratitude to the great Giver any the less, certainly.

Services in the tents were profitable, ardent prayer ascended, words of encouragement were said, and songs of praise filled the place with sweet melody.

The sermon at ten o'clock of this day was by the Rev. W. H. Alden, a Baptist clergyman, from Albany, N. Y. Text, 1 John iii. 1: "Behold what manner of love the Father hath bestowed upon us, that we should be called the sons of God." Rev. Frederick Upham, D. D., of Taunton Central Church, of more than forty years' experience in the ministry, was the preacher of the afternoon. His text was, "I that speak in righteousness, mighty to save." Isa. lxiii. 1.

Theme, "Christ the Author of our salvation." Near the close of the day, rich music of human voices — the best kind the world affords — rose on the still air from several groups assembled in different localities. The Rev. Henry Baylies, of the Fall River First Church, preached in the evening to the largest congregation of the week thus far. Text, 2 Tim. iv. 7 : "I have fought the good fight." Following the sermon, ardent prayer was heard ringing through the grove, reminding one of other fervent utterances heard here in other years. We trusted then that it would be apparent that "prayer ardent entered heaven," and that men would be made better in answer thereto. The ringing of the bell at the hour of ten cut short the work of earnest vocal worship; but we thought the employment of praise in the heaven of the saved will not be thus arrested.

Saturday, Father Tillinghast, as for a series of years, regularly, made his appearance, and addressed the children, pledging all of them he could against the use of tobacco.

The preaching of the day was by Rev. Micah J. Talbot, of Bristol, R. I., on "Who loved us, and gave himself for us;" by Rev. William McDonald, of Providence, on "Be ye therefore perfect, even as your Father which is in heaven is perfect;" and in the evening by Rev. Seth Reed, of Edgartown, to a large mass of people, on "But ye denied the Holy One and the Just, and desired a murderer to be granted unto you; and killed the Prince of Life, whom God hath raised from the dead."

The last speaker described, in telling words, the strange choice which the Jews made on that occasion. He answered the question, Why was this choice? thus: Because they were like us. If we are surprised at the choice of the Jews to release Barabbas instead of Christ, so should we be much more surprised at our choice in rejecting religion and choosing irreligion. The sermon made a powerful impression on the vast assembly. Speaking, prayer, and singing continued something like an hour, chiefly under the lead of Dr. and Mrs. Palmer, of New York, who have been so noted of late years in the promotion of revivals, both in this country and in Europe. There was present in the large audience that still remained, participating in the exercises or witnessing them, much of the spirit of revival. Several persons presented themselves for prayers.

The Sabbath. The weather was still favorable. The Love Feast, at eight o'clock, was a season of great excellence. The opening prayer was by Rev. John B. Gould, of Providence. What religious meeting on earth can surpass in interest a Methodist Camp-meeting Love Feast!

A large congregation of Christian men and women, animated by the gospel truths they have been hearing proclaimed for several successive days, and revived by answers to earnest prayers offered for a better state of mind, would be likely to enter into the duties with uncommon energy and zest. Thus it was. Ninety-four short testimonies were given, interspersed with about twenty songs of praise, occupying about an hour and a half. And the pith and force of many of the speeches or testimonies, and the soul-stirring power of those songs, swelling up from such a chorus of voices, — many of them well trained, — inspired with the hopes of heaven of which they sing, cannot be fully understood without being heard and witnessed. Such was the season of worship in which ministers and people, and Christians of all names, could participate.

The ten o'clock sermon was by Rev. Charles Payne, of Broad Street Church, Providence. The text was Mark viii. 36, 37 — "For what shall it profit a man if he gain the whole world and lose his own soul? Or what shall a man give in exchange for his soul?" The first thing considered was the worldly good, real or apparent, which may be gained in this world; the second, the price which men pay for it; the third, the loss.

At one o'clock the children were called to the stand and addressed by several persons interested in Sabbath schools.

By far the largest congregation was addressed in the afternoon by Rev. Robert M. Hatfield, of New York, formerly of the Providence Conference. His text was 1 Cor. iii. 21, 22 — "Therefore let no man glory in men; for all things are yours; whether Paul, or Apollos, or Cephas, or the world, or life, or death, or things present, or things to come, all are yours." The discourse was textual. Paul's inventory of the Christian's personal property was considered item by item. The possessions of Christians are not confined to the few; they are common to all Christians.

Rev. Samuel F. Upham preached in the evening. Text, Luke xvi. 31 — "If they hear not Moses and the prophets, neither will they be persuaded though one rose from the dead." No other words were needed to express the theme; and this was discussed in a manner which pressed the truth directly to the reason and consciences of men. The public services, both afternoon and evening, were protracted long after the sermons. The interest in the meetings was great throughout the day, and it cannot be doubted that much good was accomplished. About as many people were in the grove as on the Sabbath in previous years — say from eight to ten thousand.

It does not appear that there was any service at the stand on Monday forenoon. At two o'clock P. M., Rev. J. W. Willet preached from Num. x. 29. The invitation given by Moses to Hobab was pressed by the preacher on the attention of those who were friendly to the church, the Bible, and religion, but who were not really

Christians. The excuses of such for not becoming identified fully with the Lord's people were very thoroughly disposed of.

In the evening the people gathered at the stand for the last public service. The meeting was given into the hands of Dr. and Mrs. Palmer, to conduct it according to their own views of things. It was a truly interesting service, particularly from the fact that it was the closing one of this great occasion.

During this camp-meeting the usual business of the Association was attended to. John C. Scott, Esq., of Millville, had been appointed Chorister, and the officers of the Association had been chosen for the year. John Kendrick, William B. Lawton, Lot Phinney, and Noah Tripp were chosen a Committee on Conveyance for the next year, and required to give due notice of their arrangements for transportation of persons and baggage, in the Zion's Herald, and in one or more secular papers in Providence and New Bedford. It was voted that the Finance Committee be authorized to make such improvements and repairs as in their judgment will conduce to the best interest of the camp-meeting the coming year. Sundry alterations were made in the Articles of Agreement, especially in the Second Article, relating to membership. Also the number of members necessary to form a quorum for the transaction of business was fixed at twenty-one. Various subjects of interest were discussed. It was voted that the camp-meeting next year commence on Thursday, and close on the following Thursday.

In its purely religious traits this had been a good camp-meeting. There was a good spirit of true devotion manifest. There were some conversions, although not so many as in some other years. There had been present, more or less of the time, about a hundred ministers of the gospel, mostly Methodists. Very much of the spirit of Christian harmony prevailed.

It is true that the physical and social benefits were now added to the religious to a degree unsought for in the early years of the meeting. We do not speak of this as being wrong. We do not think it is. We think it is right, and a good thing, if persons, having the time to spare from their business, take a vacation in the heated term, and sojourn here for a while. Dwelling for a few weeks in this rural retreat, beneath the shade of these grand old oaks, hallowed by precious memories of the past, mingling with our friends, enjoying ourselves rationally, and religiously too, who will pretend to say this is inconsistent with the sanctities of the place, even though the sojourners avail themselves of the excellent privileges of sea-bathing, and walking to quaff the invigorating sea-breezes. Is not health a blessing, which, as Christians, we are bound to preserve and promote? And even though business press us, and we think we have not the time to spare, should we not take the time for such a purpose, and that at a season when we most need relaxation and rest? Men — Christian men — who have the means do take this season of the year for a vacation, and many without scruple go to Saratoga, Niagara Falls, or to some similar resort, from which they return with depleted wallets, and, very likely, considering the kind of society they meet at such resorts, with, to say the least, no more religious principle and enjoyment than they went with. We, of course, admit that many have tents and cottages here who are not professors of experimental religion, and not a few who are not connected with Methodist congregations at home; but they are usually people of high respectability, of good morals and character. And, coming to a place which they know is selected and held for religious purposes, they conform themselves to its prescribed rules, so that even during the weeks spent here before the time of the camp-meeting proper, Christian people who are here are the controlling element in the society of the place, holding frequent evening prayer-meetings, and having preaching on the holy Sabbath. How much better, then, for the Christian man, who can go somewhere to recruit his health, and as a respite from care, to come to such a place, aside from the privilege of the meeting proper, thus promoting both health and spirituality, than to go at four times the cost to either of the popular resorts named!

Then there is here the annual religious festival of about a week. Here order reigns. The police are equal to any emergency; but, to the praise of the people be it spoken, these officials have but little occasion for strong measures. Then the many excellent sermons, the earnest praying, the unsurpassed singing, are all soul-inspiring. Many Christians receive great accessions to their spiritual strength. And some souls still are awakened and converted here. And with the admission fresh upon our lips that there is, doubtless, relatively, too great a tendency to rustication here, even on the part of Christians, and not enough, relatively, of earnest labor for the salvation of souls, yet is not this a favorable place to bring men to Christ? and is there not far greater effort to that end here than in our communities at home?

CHAPTER VIII.

CAMP-MEETING OF 1865.

COULD the fathers who preached at the camp-meetings held in Wesleyan Grove some thirty years ago revisit the place now, they would hardly be able to identify the spot, except from its surroundings, which was then so consecrated and hallowed.

As this is a compend of the history of this place, as well as of the religious meetings held here, we must of course speak somewhat from year to year of the improvements in advance of those of preceding years, although it be at the expense of an appearance, at least, of repeating expressions of renewed admiration. As there is a continued endeavor on the part of the Association and its officers to make the fixtures and arrangements more and more convenient and attractive, and as the enterprise and taste of very many individuals on their own account lead them either to beautify and render more valuable their old habitations, or build new and more ornate ones, it is natural, and a matter of course, that reporters find, from year to year, some new features of the place which surpass all similar conditions of things at the times of preceding meetings. It is not strange, indeed, that we should connect with this improved state of things an increased excellence of the meetings themselves over that of some former years; for we are all apt to forget the past in our exuberance of joy at the blessings of the present.

Some of the localities in this grove have been alluded to in preceding chapters; but we wish to trace progress as we proceed in our account, and will, therefore, refer to a few of the more noted sections of interest, as they existed at the time. County Street Park was in the more northerly part of the ground, and was a delightful place. Near it was Fourth Street Avenue, much frequented. More central, and near the principal area, was Cottage Avenue, on Upham's Hill, which had all the charms of a little park, and was approached by Fisk and Park

Avenues. As elsewhere mentioned, directly south of the main circle, was Trinity Park, connecting with two entrances, or roads, to the ground, and with Broadway. A little south of this was Lincoln Park, a place of great comfort in a warm day. And still farther in the same direction was what was, for a while, called Cottage Park, now Forest Circle, being circular in shape, and surrounded by a regular system of avenues. On most of the locations named, there were, as in some other parts of the ground, beautiful cottages erected at a cost of from one hundred to seven hundred dollars, and some of the best of them furnished in much the same style as are home parlors. Some twelve to fifteen had been built this year. In drawing lines, arranging parks and avenues, and laying out lots, however, some of the old settlers, who thought the locations of their humble dwellings to be *in perpetuam*, had the misfortune to be removed from their endeared spots to others less enjoyable. As in a growing city, the old wooden building, store, and even church, must give place to the more massive structures of stone and brick, so in this city in the woods, if not by walls of granite, yet, very possibly, our house of cloth will be doomed to be superseded by one of wood, rising in architectural beauty.

Progress was also indicated this year by the better arrangements for boarding. Mr. Cady, the well-known caterer for Providence people, had erected a large two-story wooden building, the first floor of which was for an eating-room, and the second for lodging-rooms. Mr. Shove also, of Fall River, had provided a wood-covered house for those who came to his well-set tables. Other large establishments have followed in the same line since.

But while so much was being done for the comfort of the physical man, there was a growing solicitude, on the part of many, lest the plenitude of these provisions should greatly detract from the degree of spirituality manifest on these occasions in by-gone years. Hence there was an earnest endeavor to have all the means at hand to contribute to the spiritual good of the people.

It will have been observed that neither the day of the week nor that of the month had been uniform as the time appointed for the commencement of the regular camp-meeting services in this grove. That of the latter depended very much upon the time of the moon, — light nights being preferred, — and that of the former varying to suit the convenience, and, perhaps, in some cases, the *imaginary* benefits to accrue. It will have been noticed that the meeting is almost, if not quite, always held in the month of August, and that the more frequent day of the week for commencing is Tuesday. This year, however, it had been fixed for Thursday, August 10.

The splendid steamer Monohansett, which had been for a year or two in the employment of the government, having been returned to her route between New Bedford and Edgartown, and there being other boats in the vicinity, the multitudes found ample conveyance.

On the evening of the day named, the first regular religious service was held at the stand, which consisted of singing, prayer, and addresses from Revs. E. A. Lyon, of Newport, Mr. Humphriss, an aged member of the Philadelphia Conference, Mr. McCarty, of Providence, and Rev. Paul Townsend, of the Providence District.

A larger proportion than usual of the ministers present were strangers here, quite a number of whom preached. The weather was so favorable throughout this meeting, that preaching at the stand was not prevented in a single instance. The names of those who preached, in the order in which they came, were as follows: Friday, Revs. J. H. James, of Fall River, A. N. Bodfish, of North Dighton, and Mr. Kandig, of Upper Iowa Conference; Saturday, Rev. Messrs. Kinnan, of the North Indiana Conference, Trefren, of Austin, Nevada, and Seth Reed, of Edgartown; Sabbath, Rev. Drs. Wentworth, of Troy, N. Y., M. L. Scudder, of Hartford, Conn., and Rev. J. H. Twombly, of Lynn; Monday, Prof. Hibben, of the Naval Academy at Newport, R. I., Rev. D. H. Ela, of Pawtucket, and Rev. S. F. Upham, of Lowell; Tuesday, Rev. M. M. Parkhurst, of Woburn, Rev. G. M. Hamlen, of Providence Power Street Church, and Rev. A. A. Wright, of St. Paul's Church, Fall River; Wednesday, Rev. G. W. Quereau, Principal of a Seminary in the

West, Rev. B. W. Gorham, of Lynn, and Rev. Lewis B. Bates, of Millville. All the sermons were good. God's word was with power and in much assurance. The preaching was usually followed up by other public exercises at the stand. The tent. prayer-meetings were good, and a spirit of devotion was prevalent. Earnest efforts were put forth for the conversion of others, and with some success, although not so great as was desired. Several persons went forward at the stand for prayers; some were converted. One thing was becoming more and more apparent, viz., that whatever might be the disposition of people to rusticate here before and after the camp-meeting, the week of that meeting was sacredly set apart for religious work; and it was not desirable that any persons, especially Christians, should visit the place during that week with any different understanding.

The officers of the Camp-meeting Association were nearly the same as last year. President, Rev. Paul Townsend; Secretary, H. Vincent; Treasurer, Jeremiah Pease; Agent, S. P. Coffin; Finance Committee, William B. Lawton, John Kendrick, Perez Mason, P. M. Stone, H.

T. Stone, J. Remington, A. L. Westgate, R. C. Brown, Noah Tripp, C. L. Ellis, Joseph Clark, William Hathaway, J. C. Scott, James Davis, Jeremiah Pease.

There was this year made some further revision of the "Articles of Agreement."

The grounds occupied here for the purposes of the camp-meeting for so many years had now been purchased, and William B. Lawton, Abner L. Westgate, Caleb L. Ellis, and Kilborn Smith were authorized to take and hold the deeds of the same in trust for the Camp-meeting Association. The cost of the grove, rights of way, &c., was thirteen hundred dollars; and Brothers William B. Lawton, John Kendrick, and Charles H. Titus were appointed a Committee to raise the amount on the ground. At a subsequent session, the Committee reported that they had raised the requisite amount, and two hundred and fifteen dollars in excess, which last-named sum was, by their recommendation, voted to be used with other moneys which might be raised for the purpose, in making improvements on the ground. It was stated that this entire amount of fifteen hundred and fifteen dollars was raised among the cottage owners; and a hearty vote of thanks to the generous donors was passed by the Association. It was stated that more than one hundred lots had been selected on which to build tents and cottages the following year.

At one of the business meetings, the following resolution was passed with great unanimity: —

"*Resolved*, that the thanks of this Association be tendered to His Excellency Governor Andrew for calling the attention of the Chief Constable to a request sent from persons connected with this camp-meeting; to Colonel William S. King, Chief Constable of the Commonwealth, and to the five Deputy Constables of the Commonwealth detailed by the Chief for their aid in keeping order on this ground during this camp-meeting, and the very prompt and efficient manner in which they have performed this highly acceptable service." The best of order had been maintained.

During the encampment, a meeting of ministers and laymen was called together in the large business room for the special purpose of taking into consideration the propriety of holding a

New England Methodist Convention to promote various interests of the church. When assembled, the members quite unanimously expressed themselves favorable to the measure, and a Committee was appointed to prepare and report resolutions on the subject. At an adjournment next morning the Committee reported, subjects were selected to be recommended for consideration at such Convention, should one be held, and a recommendation to other camp-meetings about to be held in New England to take similar action adopted. Although the subject had been talked of in various parts, this, so far as the action of brethren at camp-meetings was concerned, was the first among the doings which resulted in the great Convention of ministers and laymen in Boston, in June of the following year.

One morning near the close of the meeting, while our venerable " Friend " Tillinghast was in the midst of his address to the children, there was an alarm of fire in the woods a short distance from the encampment. On ringing the bell, it was soon apparent that the people had not all gone home. The fire was found to be spreading, and had already extended over about a quarter of an acre of ground; but, by prompt attention in the use of such means as were at hand, it was soon arrested and extinguished, and the children's orator proceeded to finish his address, and bestow his little presents. The fire was believed to have been the work of incendiaries for plunder on the ground. But it was so quickly mastered that they were entirely foiled.

The public service of Wednesday was the last of this meeting, although some of the sojourners continued to tarry here for some days after. It was determined in one of the business meetings that the camp-meeting of next year should begin on Monday evening, and close on Tuesday morning of the following week.

One occurrence merits a word here. A large fleet of yachts, said to have been from New York, had been spending some time in this vicinity. On Sabbath evening, while they were lying in the harbor near by, there was fired from them a succession of heavy guns, occupying a considerable portion of the time of preaching, greatly annoying the worshippers. The hour of public worship must have been known. Thus to annoy a large gathering of Christian worshippers was unprincipled; to do it on a Sabbath evening was impiety. The yachtmen were probably of the more wealthy, as usual, and doubtless claim to be gentlemen. But, in the judgment of candor, the act, uncalled for as it was, was as ungentlemanly as it was unchristian.

The camp-meeting which had had a good beginning, had progressed well. The weather had been beautiful, the grove had been in its best dress, and the parks, areas, and avenues had been thronged by living, moving masses of humanity. It would be no uncommon thing to witness a gathering of ten thousand people on a city common; but to see the same number, or even half of it, gathered here in this isolated grove, is a scene more novel. There must have been an object in instituting such a meeting, and it is well known that that object was a worthy one. At the present time even Christian people — many of them, at least — visit the place for other and somewhat different purposes than the primary one, yet highly justifiable objects.

Relaxation from business cares, health, friendly greetings, — all are consistent with the Christian character — nay, of themselves, are Christian duties. If such is the fact, should we not seek the best locations for the attainment of the object? And where, as elsewhere said, on the whole New England coast, can a more salubrious or enchanting spot be found than this? Gentlemen of all ranks, and from widely different sections of the country, are confessed admirers of the grove, the arrangements, the buildings, and are especially impressed by the good order maintained.

But, while it has these advantages, it is free from many disadvantages of the Newports, Nahants, and Saratogas. It is under Christian control, and is bound to continue so. Wicked people visit here; so they do all places of public assemblies, however sacred and honored. But one great encouragement is, that many persons who come hither — the high in social position as well as the low — will sometimes listen to a gospel sermon, who seldom, if ever, do so in the church of God at home.

CHAPTER IX.

CAMP-MEETING OF 1866.

AS remarked in preceding chapters, we must note the progress made. This must be done as it relates to the improvements in and about the grounds, — the additional acquisitions, the increased number of tents and buildings, and the improved styles of them, as well as the furnishings within; likewise the increased accommodations for such as have no family domicile. In order to show on what a scale these changes were carried on for months before the meeting, even as early as the year of which we are writing, an epitome is here given of the result of observations made upon the ground, August 6. In the early years, those who came to encamp did not arrive till on or near the day of beginning. They came for purely spiritual objects, not for pleasure. After the lapse of years, when family tents came in vogue, some few persons came a few days, or perhaps a week, preceding the meeting, to enjoy the luxury of this short sojourn, an important feature of which was a clam-bake. But it is not till within a few years that large numbers have come several weeks before the commencement for recreation. They began to come this year by the 10th of July. There were now (August 6) about one hundred families here, besides sixty carpenters and painters, who were busy as bees, from early morn till dewy eve, erecting and beautifying these rural homes.

The first wooden building designed as a family residence was that of Rev. Frederick Upham, put up some ten or twelve years previous, and was only about ten by twelve feet. The number of wooden buildings increased but slowly at first, although they were yearly improving in style and size. They were now the rage. They cost, at that time, from two to seven hundred dollars; average, about four hundred dollars. Many then, as now, were furnished in the style of home parlors. Some fifty had been put up this year, and still the work was going on. There were already persons owning cottages here from five different states. Among the many fine ones were those of Dr. Moses L. Scudder, of Hartford, Ct.; Lawton and Mason, of Providence, R. I.; William Hathaway, of Dighton, Mass.; and Mrs. Richmond Bullock, of Providence. Increased accommodations were made for the lodging of strangers, and such as had no family domicile. Among them was Mr. Dunbar's two-and-a-half story building, in the eastern part of the ground.

Important changes had been made in some of the avenues, and boarding establishments had been moved to make room for the beautiful cottages. Mr. Washburn, of Acushnet, had had his "Prairie" boarding-house reconstructed somewhat in the style of Mr. Cady's, of the previous year. There were now daily arrivals, in considerable numbers, by the steamer, with baggage, freight, and large quantities of lumber required for new buildings. Some three or four boarding establishments were already open. A store, and other provisions to accommodate housekeepers, were at hand. Walking, bathing, and other recreations, were enjoyed, and religious meetings often held. Sabbath services were regular. The place was under Christian control.

On the 11th of the month, a visit to the ground showed that work was going on with spirit. The numbers now here were counted by the thousands. Formerly we came here for the benefit of the soul only; now we come for the improvement of the casket of the soul, and for the cultivation of the social elements, as well. The merchant, the student, and the invalid were here. The means of recuperation and the boon of health were here. We had not the luxuries, nor the "congress water;" but we had what was quite as useful as the furnishings at Saratoga, and at far less rates; and then we were under better influences.

Additional grounds had been purchased, a new wharf had been built by Messrs. Luce & Littlefield, and a new road opened thereto from the camp. Among the builders engaged here were Messrs. Henry and Cornelius Ripley, Charles Worth, Freeman Pease, Ellis Lewis, and many others. The men who wrought with the paint-brush followed the builders in quick succession. Of these were Messrs. Edward Smith, William Goff, and a Mr. West.

Coming down to the time near the beginning of the camp-meeting, we find, among the rusticators, Rev. Sidney Dean, late an M. C., now editor of the Providence "Press," and the Rev. Mr. Twombly, of the N. E. Conference.

Among the families sojourning here, there were many children, who were occasionally gathered at the stand for speaking and singing, performing their part to the admiration of D. Ds., and many others present.

The Sabbath preceding the commencement was a very enjoyable day. The morning prayers, at eight o'clock, were conducted by Rev. Dr. F. Upham, of Newport, R. I. The forenoon sermon was by Rev. Mr. Thomas, of Bristol, R. I. The Rev. Dr. Scudder, of Hartford, Ct., was to preach at the stand in the afternoon; but the afternoon proving rainy, he preached in one of the large tents. Prof. Stowe was one of the hearers, and followed the preacher in some well-timed remarks. At the same hour there was preaching in two other tents by Rev. R. M. Hatfield, of Chicago, and

Rev. Mr. Andrew, of Stamford, Conn. The last two gentlemen were of a yacht party of twenty-six, mostly clergymen, from New York and vicinity, making a summer trip in these and neighboring waters. Rev. Prof. Stowe, also Dr. Crook, editor of the "Methodist," Rev. Mr. Woodruff, of New York, Rev. Dr. Tiffany, of Chicago, and others well known, were of the party. There were judged to be about three thousand people in the grove on the Sabbath mentioned.

Steamboats were abundant, and people were coming in large numbers. A daily mail was established for the meeting, as usual.

At the first public exercise of the regular series, about two thousand people came to the seats to hear. As is frequently the case of late years, at this opening service there were several addresses, instead of a set sermon.

At a meeting of the Camp-meeting Association, a short time preceding the public service named, the Rev. Dr. Samuel C. Brown, Presiding Elder of the Providence District, had been chosen President of the Association, which also gave him the superintendence of this camp-meeting. This first public service was, therefore, conducted by him. In the opening, he gave out the seven hundred and seventh hymn, —

> " And are we yet alive,
> And see each other's face ? " &c.;

and then offered an earnest and appropriate prayer, followed by singing the seven hundred and twenty-fifth hymn, and the reading of select portions of Scripture. The doctor then proceeded to address the assembly. We had met for the purpose of a Methodist camp-meeting. By whatever name others might be disposed to designate the gathered multitude in this place, he claimed that it was strictly what he had now pronounced it. It was to be a Methodist camp-meeting, conducted according to Methodist usages. Not that we would be sectarian in any exceptional sense, for we extend to all, of all names, a most cordial welcome.

The doctor continued in an appropriate strain, and was followed by Dr. Upham, of Newport, Rev. L. B. Bates, of New Bedford, and Rev. S. F. Upham, son of the doctor. Rev. Dr. Scudder closed in an earnest prayer.

August 21. This was a good day both for

those who were permanently here, and for those who came only for the day, as many did. The sun was bright, the air salubrious, and the walking agreeable. Several of the Deputy State Constables were in attendance, and the ordinary police force was organized. There was the usual good order observable from the first. Rev. James D. Butler, of Providence, was the preacher of the forenoon. Rev. Joseph H. James, of Fall River, and Rev. John Allen, of Maine, followed in addresses. In the afternoon Rev. Robert M. Hatfield, of Chicago, preached a sermon on the subject of the "Resurrection." Text, Phil. iii. 21. Rev. Mr. Woodruff, before named, followed in an earnest and eloquent address.

Among the eminent personages visiting the ground during the day were Rev. Dr. Abel Stevens, of New York, the great historian of Methodism; the Captain of the School Ship, which is anchored in the harbor near by; the Hon. Alexander H. Rice, M. C., of the Third District, and Judge Russell, of the Superior Court. All laud the place. Who could do otherwise? A cordial greeting of the first named of the above list awakened memories of incidents when at a seminary together, and he, then a boy of scarcely sixteen years, was the most eloquent and popular preacher in all the region.

August 22. The weather being stormy, our "Friend" held his meeting in the morning with the children in the New Bedford Pleasant Street tent. Among other things, a wide-awake Sabbath School Superintendent from Worcester gave the history of a pear which was repeatedly sold for a benevolent object till the aggregate of sales was about thirty dollars, and of a three-cent piece which in like manner brought more than eleven dollars.

The preaching in the forenoon was in tents by Revs. Seth Reed, C. Nason, A. Palmer, J. Livesey, and J. H. Sheffield. The weather being more favorable in the afternoon, Rev. Asa N. Bodfish, of Dighton, occupied the stand; but before he had completed his sermon, a shower of rain broke up the congregation.

During the day a worthless vagrant from abroad, previously known to Deputy State Constable Coleman, of New Bedford, in attendance here, was arrested by him, and brought before Jeremiah Pease, Esq., of Edgartown, Trial Justice, and by him sentenced for sixty days in the House of Correction.

The sermon of the evening was by Rev. Lewis B. Bates, of New Bedford. Subject, "Decision." The sermon was followed, as usual, by earnest exhortation. The prayer-meetings following the public service were spirited. Vice-President Hamlin and Representative Gooch were among the distinguished visitors upon the ground during the day.

August 23. Quiet had reigned through the night, as usual, and we awoke from refreshing slumbers to greet again the glorious sunshine.

At one of the meetings of the Camp-meeting Association, the annual choice of the large Finance Committee of fifteen laymen took place. Most of them were the same as last year. They were William B. Lawton, Henry T. Stone, Pardon M. Stone, John Kendrick, James Davis, John C. Scott, Robert C. Brown, John D. Flint, Iram Smith, William L. Hathaway, J. J. Stanley, Caleb L. Ellis, Noah Tripp, J. C. Brock, and Jeremiah Pease. The powers of this Committee were much larger than its title would seem to indicate. They had a controlling influence in laying out the grounds in avenues and lots. Coming from a quiet neighboring town into this city of tents and cottages, in the main entrances to which there was so much of bustle and stir, was not unlike passing along the thoroughfares of a real city. Such was life here.

The day became lowery, notwithstanding the promising indications of the early morning. Rev. J. H. Sheffield, of Holmes Hole, attempted to preach; but drops came down, and the people scattered. They soon found, however, that they were "more scared than hurt." Rev. F. J. Wagner, of the New Bedford Allen Street Church, succeeded better in the afternoon, under the occasional sprinklings from the pending clouds, while he persevered to the close. Then a real rain set in, and we went hurriedly to our temporary homes. Rev. Messrs. King, Palmer, and Gifford preached in tents in the evening. Prayer-meetings were held in some others. In one of the latter there was quite a reunion of ex-pastors.

Preceding the afternoon sermon of to-day, two

colored students from Lincoln Seminary, in the State of Pennsylvania, — Johnson and Stevenson, — were present, the former of whom made an effective address from the stand, and a collection was taken to aid them in their education.

The 24th was a marked day in the progress of the meeting. The weather was fine throughout, although rather cool. One of the morning attractions was a meeting held by Mr. Lewis B. Loode, of New York, Superintendent of the Pacific Street Church Sabbath School in Brooklyn.

The ten o'clock sermon was by Rev. Joseph H. James, of Fall River. At one o'clock Professor Tourjee, of Providence, with a host of other singers, entertained a crowd at the stand with sacred music. Before the sermon, Rev. Charles Nason, of Scituate, made an appeal for aid for the society at that place, whose church had been consumed by fire. Rev. Mr. Humphriss, of the New Bedford County Street Church, was the preacher of the afternoon. His subject was, "The Gospel Invitation." Rev. A. W. Paige, of Edgartown, preached in the evening from

Luke xi. 28–30. Several, who came forward for prayers after the last sermon, professed conversion.

Saturday, August 25. The day was propitious. The people continued to come. One would suppose that the daily coming would, at this stage of the meeting, increase the numbers to a living mass. But they do not all come to tarry through. Very many come but for a few hours, or perhaps a day or two. Some come, doubtless, from motives of sheer curiosity; others, who have heard of the fame of the place, visit it to see for themselves what these Christian people are doing here, and perhaps with the thought of taking up a temporary residence with them. Such, and perhaps many who have no such intention, soon come to the conclusion to have a tent or a cottage here, if lots are to be had. Such has been the eagerness with which lots have been seized, that the author was informed, notwithstanding the very extensive arrangements this year, there was not a lot of the Association now to be had, and several persons had obtained sites of a private individual owning adjoining grounds. The Association had, however, broad acres not yet laid cut, which would, doubtless, soon be cleared up and put in a condition which would make them available. But notwithstanding so many come for a *very* temporary stay, thousands remain as regular denizens. During this day about four thousand people came to remain the following day.

The sermon of the forenoon was by Rev. William Livesey, of Middletown, R. I; that of the afternoon was by Rev. David H. Ela, of Providence; and that of the evening was by Rev. Samuel F. Upham, of Lowell. The congregation of the evening was large and attentive. The stillness of the night lent inspiration to the occasion, and the weighty words spoken evidently made a deep impression on many minds.

The Sabbath is always the great day as to the numbers in attendance at these annual gatherings. The freights of human beings, coming on some five or six steamers, added very greatly, of course, to the numbers already here. It was judged that about five thousand came on the several boats from New Bedford, and one thousand on the Island Home from Nantucket and the Cape. Add to these the multitudes by other conveyances, by land and water, and I think the entire number by midday could not have been less than sixteen thousand; probably it was somewhat more. Some put it at eighteen thousand.

The camp-meeting Love Feast at eight o'clock A. M. was a very memorable meeting. Over one hundred and sixty persons gave short testimonies in about an hour and a quarter. These were interspersed with rich songs of praise. Thousands were gathered, and the spirit of the meeting was excellent. Some say it was the best of the kind they ever attended.

It had been decided to hold a memorial meeting of the centenary of Methodism at ten o'clock, and the service commenced; but the heavens, about that time, were overcast, and a shower of rain sent the people to the tents, in a large number of which preaching service was held. Man appoints, but God often disappoints. His ways are best, although we do not always see it at the time. These tent meetings proved to be profitable.

At one o'clock a Sabbath School gathering was held at the stand, at which the children were addressed by Brother Maynard, a Sabbath School man from New York, and Rev. Charles Payne, of Brooklyn.

At two o'clock P. M. the deferred Centenary service took place, the weather having become very fine again. Rev. Charles H. Titus read the seventy-eighth hymn, which was sung. Prayer was offered by Rev. John D. King; select portions of Scripture were then read by the President of the meeting, — Dr. Brown, — and, after singing the nine hundred and thirty-third hymn, the same gentleman proceeded to make the introductory address to the assembled throng. He stated the object of this special service to be, to show our gratitude to Almighty God for what he had done for us and through us, as a people, within the last century, and to incite to increased zeal and effort in the cause of the divine Master. We wanted to bring up to our view the spiritual portraits of the fathers of the church, who so earnestly labored and sacrificed, for the purpose of inspiring ourselves with fresh vigor in the work to which we are called.

At the close of his remarks, the President introduced the Rev. Seth Reed, of Providence, R. I.

After some words of introduction, the speaker proceeded to give reasons at some length why we should celebrate this centenary of American Methodism. It was well to study these things. The unprecedented growth of this denomination, its churches built, its contributions to benevolent causes, its literature, its educational enterprises, its missionary and Sunday School operations, its influence on the religious consciousness of the community, and upon the theology of the country, and especially its multiplied converts to the grace of God, were topics dwelt upon in choice language, and with rare power. The address, which lasted about three quarters of an hour, was one of the happy efforts of an eminent man.

After singing the one thousand and second hymn, the Rev. Dr. Scudder, of Hartford, Conn., was introduced. He held that Methodism is of God. He could defend this position from every part of its history. He would base what he had to say on one statement: that the development of the Methodist church was the result of the religious experience of its subjects or members — the experience of the grace of God renewing the heart. For about thirty-five or forty minutes the doctor spoke with even more than his wonted power and force on this subject, elaborating it.

Immediately upon the closing of this centenary service, the thousands who came only for the day, and who had either been listening to the words of the preachers, resting in the tents and cottages, or thronging the avenues and parks, withdrew from the grounds, and wended their way homeward.

The hour of the evening service, however, showed that there were many other thousands still remaining. A large and attentive audience listened to a very able sermon pronounced by Rev. David Patten, D. D., of the Concord Biblical Institute. It was founded on several of the first verses of the thirty-third chapter of Ezekiel. It was a cogent argument, showing the principles of human responsibility and of divine retribution. There cannot be a well-ordered State without government. Government is founded on law. Law implies an ability on the part of those who are its subjects to obey it. Hence our responsibility. If we do not obey, there must be retribution. The honor of the government and the good of the governed both require the punishment of the offender. God can never give up his right to be obeyed. The only safety of the sinner is to obey and be saved.

The usual invitation and prayers followed the sermon.

On Monday, the last day, there was found to be present, notwithstanding the departures, enough to constitute an audience of very considerable size. Preaching at ten o'clock by Rev. William H. Richards, of Fall River, and at two o'clock by Rev. Charles S. McReading, of Nantucket, whose father, many years previous, was pastor of the Edgartown church.

At seven o'clock in the evening the last public meeting took place at the stand. After singing and prayer, the audience, which was large for the last one, was addressed by the President and seven other ministers, all in a strain of congratulation at the spirit and good results of this camp-meeting. It was felt that the conversions, which had occurred in considerable numbers, constituted but a single item of its good effects. The excellent order, notwithstanding the masses, the elevated Christian tone of the meeting, and, generally, its tendency to put the Martha's Vineyard Camp-meeting, and the denomination sustaining it, right before the country, were sources of gratitude. The closing prayer-meeting was powerful, and this camp-meeting, now closed, had been a great success.

As usual, during the days of the camp-meeting, there were several sessions of the Camp-meeting Association. The reports of the Finance Committee, Agent, and Treasurer, showed the financial condition to be healthy. The appointment of Agent and Treasurer was committed to the Finance Committee; and the old Secretary of the Association and of the meeting, having served in the latter capacity more than three fourths of the time since the first meeting held here, and continuously in the former ever since its formation, was now very appropriately superseded, the Rev. David H. Ela, of Providence, being chosen. Perhaps, considering the circumstances, it may be regarded as an historical fact worth preserving, that the Association very kindly voted "That the thanks of the Association be tendered to Rev. Hebron Vincent for his long and faithful services as Secretary." Also, in view of the fact that his ceasing to be an officer of the Association ended his membership of the same, it was with equal kindness voted, "That, in consideration of said services, he be made an honorary member of the Association."

A Committee, consisting of Hon. George F. Gavitt, William Mason, Kilborn Smith, Edmund Anthony, and James Rothwell, were appointed to nominate persons to hold the lands of the Association as trustees; also to have deeds made in trust for the Association; also, to apply to the Legislature of Massachusetts, at its next session, for an act of incorporation. To this Committee was also referred the subject of the taxation of cottages on this ground by the town of Edgartown.

This Committee, at a subsequent session, submitted, through their Chairman, a very full report upon the various matters referred to them, and as it was an important and well-prepared document, and the basis of much action of interest afterward, it is given here entire. It is as follows: —

"The Committee appointed by vote of the

Association, August 22, to consider and report upon various matters relating to the Association as expressed by said vote, have attended to the duty assigned them, and after careful consideration respectfully submit the following

REPORT.

"The first matter brought to the notice of your Committee was the fact that the deeds of the land occupied by the Association were, with one exception, conveyances of land to certain individuals, and not to the Martha's Vineyard Camp-meeting Association; so that, in reality, the land belonged to those individuals, and the Association had no legal title to the property whatever. This your Committee conclude to have been an oversight on the part of the persons taking the deeds, and they have accordingly given new deeds of the land, so that it is now all deeded in trust to the Martha's Vineyard Camp-meeting Association. Your Committee are satisfied that the deeds are now all right, and they would recommend that these deeds be kept by the Treasurer of the Association.

"The next subject to which the attention of your Committee was called, was the appointment of an Agent and Treasurer of the Association. After a cordial consideration of this matter, we would recommend that no change be made for the present year in these officers.

"In regard to the incorporation of the Association, your Committee think it important, and essential to the interests of the Association, that it be done as soon as practicable. But while, in our opinion, it may be done under the general laws of the State, yet the advantages of a special act of incorporation are so numerous that your Committee would recommend that application be made to the Legislature, at its next session, for a special act of incorporation.

"The matter of taxation of the cottages upon the grounds of the Association, which was referred to your Committee, has been duly considered; but we have been unable to arrive at anything definite in regard thereto. Your Committee find the authorities of the town of Edgartown disposed to do whatever is right in the premises, and entirely willing to abide any legal decision, or settle the matter in any way that shall not exceed their powers as agents of the town. It is a subject not within the province of your Committee to decide, but we would recommend that a Committee of the Association be appointed, who, with the assessors of the town, shall lay the matter before a legal tribunal for decision, each party obligating itself to abide the decision. Meanwhile the collector of taxes has received instructions to suspend the collection of taxes on the cottages until such decision be reached.

"There is another matter, which, though perhaps not within the province of your Committee to act upon, yet we deem it of sufficient importance to call the attention of the Association to the subject, in order that some action may be taken thereon. We find, in the deed of the first land bought by the Association, that there is a lease of the land to certain persons for the use of the Camp-meeting Association, which lease does not expire until 1871. This lease may work no harm to the Association, yet we think it would be much better to have it annulled; and your Committee are of the opinion that the gentlemen holding this lease would be perfectly willing to give it up.

(Signed)   GEO. F. GAVITT,
WM. MASON,
K. SMITH."

[Dated Aug. 27, 1866.]

The Report was adopted by the Association, and the same Committee were requested by vote to carry out the suggestions of the same.

In bringing to a close the account of this meeting and its doings, we would say that men of wealth were here, as well as men of grace; and although the increasing numbers resorting hither from year to year, and a wise forecast for the wants of the future, require liberal outlays, the means were at hand in abundance to meet all expenses. It was also generally understood that the grounds were not purchased for speculation, nor for any other purposes than those for which they were now being used. They were held *in trust* by Christian men for this Camp-meeting Association; and the Finance Committee of fifteen laymen, who have the principal management of affairs connected therewith, were required by the Constitution of the Association to be members of the Methodist Episcopal Church. It was designed that these grounds should remain ever, as they now were, under Christian control. The rumored offer of fifty thousand dollars by a speculator would not have been regarded as the least temptation whatever; nor would the estimate of its worth by George Francis Train, who visited the place this season, — viz., three hundred thousand dollars, — be sufficient to make Judases of the men who worship their Lord in this sacred retreat. Mr. Train, in a letter to the New York "Express," says that in ten years he could make these thirty-five acres, which he now valued as above stated, "worth three million dollars." We think that although these lands and those in the vicinity have been increasing in value since that year, yet no such fortune could ever be realized by the occupancy of these premises. Correspondingly extravagant was Mr. Train's estimate of the numbers here. He said that thirty years ago "fifty people knelt here, now fifty thousand." His letter had in it much that was good, but his laudations went beyond reason.

CHAPTER X.

CAMP-MEETING OF 1867.

WHEREVER, in this land of the Pilgrims, there is any special gathering of the people open to the public, there will be the indomitable Yankee, with his implements of some handicraft, his "notions" of trade, or his plans of some kind for turning up the dollar; or, in other words, the "greenbacks." And there, too, will be gentlemen, all ready, if the opportunity offer, for a profitable investment. In this free land, all claim the right so to do, provided they do not infringe the rights of others.

The late William Butler, Esq., who resided in Eastville, in the vicinity of what is now the camp-ground, and of whom this camp-meeting site was first leased, owned a very large tract of land hereabouts. Subsequently to his decease, and the division of his estate among his children, certain portions changed hands. By one of such transfers, a large tract of wood and cleared land, south-easterly of what is now the property of the Camp-meeting Association, and bordering on the sea on the east, passed, by purchase, to the ownership of the late Captain Shubael Norton,—it being contiguous to his homestead,—and subsequently became a part of the premises of his son, Captain Shubael L. Norton, who had now held it for quite a number of years. The open lands and the bluffs had now long been used by the campers for promenading, and the neighboring shore for sea-bathing. So wonderfully had this camp-meeting increased, and the camp itself extended, that, as elsewhere noted, additional acres had been annexed to those of the first purchase, and still, at the camp-meeting of 1866, initiatory steps were taken to negotiate the acquisition of the above-named adjoining lands of Captain Norton, or at least the woodland portion of them. By some oversight, however, the right measures had been too long delayed; for, at just about that juncture, the captain made sale of five sixths of them to as many gentlemen, reserving the other one sixth to himself. The whole of the territory thus owned contained about seventy-five acres. The owners, who were Captains Shubael L. Norton, Ira Darrow, Grafton N. Collins, and William Bradley, Esq., of Edgartown, E. P. Carpenter, Esq., of Foxboro', and William S. Hills, Esq., of Boston, formed a company, under the name of "The Land and Wharf Company;" and before the date of the camp-meeting of 1867, the cleared land, as well as the wood land, had been laid out in lots for cottages and tents. The company had also built a substantial wharf, at a cost of about five thousand dollars. They erected, near the head of their wharf, a wooden building, ninety by twenty feet, a story and a half high, the first floor of which was to be for storage, victualling, and other useful purposes, and the second for lodging-rooms, to be let. A few cottages had been built in their grove. In the central part of it was a large and beautiful one, in course of construction, for E. P. Carpenter, Esq. The wharf was but a few minutes' walk from the camp circle.

The sale of these lands to the gentlemen named gave rise, at first, to various rumors as to their intentions respecting the means they proposed to adopt for money-making, which, indeed, were represented by Madam Rumor to be so hostile to the interests of the camp-meeting as to become an annoyance to it. Under these impressions, many of those connected with the meeting, headed by the Finance Committee, were inclined to purchase the premises and wharf of the present owners, even at a great advance of price of the lands at their last sale, if in their judgment reasonable; otherwise to remove the entire camp-meeting fixtures to some other place. During this state of things new sites were examined. In close connection, as to time, with these movements, repeated conferences were held by the two parties or their respective delegates. By these conferences the authorities of the meeting became disabused as to the intentions of the company; and although they were unwilling to pay the price set upon their property, they relinquished, for the present, at least, the idea of the removal of the camp-meeting.

The members of the Land and Wharf Company were all of them highly respectable, — some of them Christian men, — and although they readily conceded that their purchase of these lands meant business, yet the methods they proposed to adopt were such, and such only, as were legitimate and honorable; designing to do nothing which should conflict with the interests of the meeting, but conforming themselves to its regulations during the days of its sessions. Still it was felt by the Association that there was not a harmony of interests. This camp-meeting was established for purely religious objects. Its members came not here for purposes of worldly gain, but, on the other hand, sacrificed much of time and means to promote the worship of God, and benefit, spiritually, the people who assembled there,—although it is true these gatherings have in a measure changed, partaking more of a social character than at the first. But the governing influence and object are still religious, and the camp-meeting proper remains, and ever will remain, the central attraction and force of all gathering and visiting here as a summer resort even. It did, therefore, seem hard to the members of the Association and others interested with them in the worship here, that gentlemen whose contiguous lands would never have been worth a tithe of their purchase money but for this religious meeting, should avail themselves of the opportunity to plant by their side a large interest so diverse in its nature and object. It was this, even after explanations had been made, which engendered and nurtured feelings of dissatisfaction on the part of the Association, and of opposition, in some sense, between the two parties. But we must now look at the condition of things in all their bearings. The arrangements on both sides of the line were fixed facts. Costly building was progressing, indicating permanence. There could be nothing gained, but everything vitiated, by unfriendly words or acts. A measure of harmony, it is believed, has since been obtained; and most certainly it is the interest of all to act the part of good Christians, as well as good philosophers, and, whatever may be the merits of the case, abide resignedly by the condition of things we cannot help.

One thing seemed to be settled beyond a peradventure — that no present or prospective want of harmony between the two, nor between the Association and any other neighboring landowner, could have the least tendency to unsettle the permanency of this encampment, or of the religious camp-meetings held here. There was too much property here, to say nothing of attachments to the place, to surrender, for any ordinary cause, the privileges and blessings of this beautiful city, the admiration of all visitors to the spot; and it was hoped that, in some way, there would be an amicable termination of all pending differences, however slight, that there might remain nothing to disturb the Christian equanimity of the thousands who congregate and temporarily dwell here. It is true the jostling may be but slight; but for the good of all concerned, there had better be none at all.

Notwithstanding the disturbing elements referred to, and notwithstanding that, on account of the same, there had been thought to be some uncertainty as to the continuance of the camp-meetings here beyond the current year, still, for a month or two before the time appointed for the commencing of this year's camp-meeting, there was much evidence of surviving life. Facts of interest accumulated. There had been, within the time named, a constantly increasing amount of travel between this place and New Bedford and the regions beyond. Many came to tarry for the season, others for a short time. Not a few gentlemen brought their families, but left them occasionally for a flying visit home on business, and then returned. Some clergymen found it pleasant to rusticate here in the week time, and then spend the Sabbath with their parishioners, returning here when the Sabbath toils were over. And some of them, who came to rest from their work at home, found here a people ready and anxious to hear the word of the Lord from their lips. There had been preaching here for the five preceding Sabbaths. The pleasure-seekers, mechanics, and laborers turned out in respectable numbers. The Rev. Mr. Whitaker, of Lowell, came hither, by permission of his people, to rest, and yet yielded to the desires of his new associates to preach once on a Sabbath for three successive Sabbaths. The people, in appreciation of his services, took up for him, on the third Sabbath, a handsome collection. Of this, several who were not of the same faith, but were sojourners here, claimed to do a part. It was estimated, a week before the meeting, that there were from twelve to fifteen hundred people in the grove. There were some fifty to sixty mechanics finding full employment. A nice cottage, with its appendages, was raised and finished in a very few days.

While walking, fishing, bathing, and the like activities gave edge to the appetite, there was no lack of provision made to meet the demands of the inner man. There were good boarding establishments ready to receive customers, and there were also stores and a market prepared to supply various needfuls to those who preferred to set their own tables in their quiet domiciles. Boating on the pond near by had become one of the prominent means of exercise and pastime.

When, on the Friday preceding the meeting, the author had become quartered in a comfortable habitation, he looked out upon the grounds, the beautiful dwellings, the costly arrangements, and the business accompaniments so necessary to the comfort of the sojourner, and asked himself, "Is it a reality? Am I really in the old Wesleyan Grove? or am I in some fairy-land? It must be the same place; but, O, how changed! The old oak forest, which I entered, with a few others, about thirty-two years ago, for the purpose of selecting a spot for the camp-meeting site, has been cleared of underbrush, and become densely populated over broad acres. Instead of the few hundreds of poor, humble followers of the Master, who came here to worship, dwelling in rough tents, we have now, it is true, a remnant, a sprinkling of these, but mostly those of fashion, and many of large wealth." It was estimated that the combined wealth of those having cottages and tents here would amount to several millions of dollars. And they were now of several denominations, and some of no denomination.

For the five weeks preceding the meeting, the travel and transportation of baggage and freight had been increasing, till now there was what might be called a rush.

On the Sabbath next preceding the meeting, large numbers were in the grove. Rev. Lewis B. Bates, of New Bedford, preached in the forenoon. In the afternoon there was a children's meeting, which was presided over by Dr. M. L. Scudder, and addressed by several distinguished gentlemen. There was a sermon in the evening, by Rev. Allen A. Gee, Presiding Elder of the Nashville District, in Tennessee. The long spell of rainy and foggy weather had subsided, and the light beamed in upon us on this holy day with all the quiet and stillness desirable at a time so sacred; and such were the scenes and ceremonies that the casual observer could hardly distinguish between this and one of the regular camp-meeting days, except that, it being the Sabbath, it was more quiet, of course, than one of the week days of the meeting.

The day of commencing this camp-meeting was Monday, August 12. At four o'clock of this day, croqueting, which had been much practised, and all the other features of recreation, were ordered to cease in the grove for the week, and during camp-meeting days. The ease with which this change took place, showed how readily orderly people can pass from what is strictly social and secular, to a condition characterized by sacred ceremonies.

It was early announced that Philip Phillips, the celebrated Christian vocalist, was expected here on the day of beginning. As sacred song is a very considerable part of the power of the church, it was expected that his visit here would not be in vain. Picture-makers were here by the half-dozen. Our prayer was, that the moral artists, who were also here in force, would so clearly daguerreotype truth upon the hearts of the people, that all the hearers thereof would " know themselves."

Opening exercises of the regular series were held at the stand in the evening of this first day, favored by delightful weather. Addresses by Dr. Brown, the Superintendent of the camp-meeting, and several other clergymen.

One marked characteristic of the camp-meetings held in this far-famed grove has ever been the excellent order and decorum prevailing here. Occasionally, wayward sons are seen about the grounds; but such soon become penetrated by the conviction that good behavior is their greatest safeguard. We have always had law officers who are friendly to the objects of the meeting; and if any persons are disposed to be unruly, they soon become satisfied that, being on an island, it would not be easy to escape detection. Not knowing, however, what wicked men might be tempted to do, we have ever thought it well, since the meeting has become large, to have a strong police force in attendance. For the last few years Deputy State Constables had been detailed to assist in the maintenance of the decorums of the place. The present year we had four of these; viz., Mr. Jason L. Dexter, of Edgartown, chief, William C. Thomas, of New Bedford, Charles H. Morton, of Fairhaven, and William D. Tripp, of Taunton. In addition to these, and other civil officers on the ground, there was constituted a day police force of twelve, and a night police of six. With these provisions we had very little concern about thieves or pickpockets, or any other class of evil-doers. We rested quietly.

At a meeting of the Association, Samuel C. Brown, D. D., was chosen President, and Rev. David H. Ela, Secretary.

Many persons visiting this ground from time to time to ask for charity, and the frequent public presentation of such cases proving an annoyance to the people, a Committee of five was raised, to whom all such cases should be referred. The following resolution was adopted by the Committee: —

"*Resolved*, That we cannot encourage the public presentation of cases for private charity on this camp-ground, with the exception of those of personal suffering."

Of course, gifts could be received here as elsewhere.

On the second day, Rev. J. W. Willet, of Rockville, Ct., was the preacher in the forenoon. Text, Luke xxiv. 49. Theme, the Gift of Power which was to be received by the Apostles,

Preceding the sermon of the afternoon, the Rev. Mr. Gee, to whom I have before made reference, presented, in an earnest speech, the condition of things in Central Tennessee. He alluded to the rebellion, and the rebellious element still smouldering in the ruins of the fallen confederacy. The Freedmen's Aid Society had done much for education in that state; but it was hoped that the system of free schools would be so fully in force in a year or two, as to be able to dispense with aid from that friendly source. But they wanted help for a more advanced institution. They were about founding a college there to educate young men for ministers and teachers. It was called the Central Tennessee

Methodist Episcopal College. Rev. Mr. Mallalieu, of Boston, had been invited to become its President.

The sermon of the afternoon was by Rev. Mr. Stanley, of the New Bedford Fourth Street Church. The evening service consisted mainly of addresses by Dr. James Porter, of the New York Book Agency, Rev. John H. Twombly, Rev. Dr. Upham, and Rev. J. D. King; followed by a season of prayer for seekers of religion, one of whom afterward found relief to his mind in one of the tents.

The sermons of the third day were by Rev. L. D. Davis, and Rev. Mr. Bowler, of Fall River, since deceased. The preacher of the forenoon was followed by Rev. Charles K. True, D. D., in an eloquent address, tracing out the thoughts contained in the sermon; and the sermon of the afternoon was, in like manner, followed by an effective appeal to the unconverted by Rev. V. A. Cooper, of Providence. The third service of the day was similar to that of the previous evening.

Large numbers of people had arrived by the steamers; among them, Mr. Phillips, the vocalist, who charmed the people with his fine vocal music, accompanied by that of his cabinet organ.

Thursday. The weather continued fine. Before the commencement of the ten o'clock service, Mr. Phillips, with his corps of singers about him, gave us some rich preludes. He favored us many times, in a similar way, afterward. The sermon was by Dr. James Porter, of New York, before named. That of the afternoon was by Prof. William H. Perrine, of Albion College, Michigan.

In a private conversation, Mr. Perrine informed the author that this place was not understood at the West. He was collecting material from the descriptions of the location, the history of the camp-meetings held here, and any other sources of information, to present a true view to his Western friends. The gentleman was like all others who visit the encampment: whatever may have been their prejudices against it, they are charmed by its beauty, and go forth to speak its praise. The fact is, taking all things into account, the outlay in its fixtures and habitations, and the combined benefits of its gatherings of the people, there is nothing like it, nor equal to it, of the camp-meeting kind, in all the world.

The evening sermon was by Rev. V. A. Cooper, of Providence.

Friday. A slight rain fell during the preceding night, and the morning was somewhat lowery, but not enough so to prevent service at the stand. Prayer and praise arose, as usual, from many a company at the morning hour. The sermon at ten o'clock was by Rev. Aaron D. Sargent, of the New England Conference. The writer's first recollections of him were associated with camp-meeting scenes in the neighboring town of Falmouth, more than forty years ago. He was then a hale young man; now, venerable with years. Camp-meeting John Allen followed the preacher in some remarks, in which he referred to the Vineland Camp-meeting, which he had lately attended. Rev. Dr. Lane, and several others, also addressed some words to the people. The preacher of the afternoon was Rev. Dr. Rust, of Cincinnati. Near the close of the sermon, a shower dispersed the congregation.

At the usual hour at evening, a large audience

assembled at the stand to listen to a sermon from Dr. True. The preliminary services were gone through, and the President of the meeting was about to introduce the speaker, when the indications of an immediate rain were so manifest, that the people were allowed to leave the seats, preaching being announced at the large County Street tent by Dr. True. There was also preaching to crowds of people in the New Bedford Pleasant Street tent, the Pawtucket tent, and the Mathewson Street, Providence, tent. The speakers were Rev. Messrs. Wagnor, Willet, and Perrine. As yet, not many had professed conversion, but the services were becoming deeply interesting.

Saturday. The clouds had passed over, and the sun shone brightly again. The floating thousands of people had been coming and going; but the ingress was now far greater than the egress. Most of those who come so late in the week do so with the intention of spending the Sabbath here. With the crowds of other classes came a sprinkling of the "cloth" and of the press. Boston papers, as usual, have their men here. Providence and New Bedford, and other neighboring cities, do not overlook their interests, and New York is not without its representative. Then there are gentlemen here from far-off cities who will furnish letters to their neighboring papers. The island paper, of course, takes notes. Last, but not least, as for several years, the "Camp-Meeting Herald," a daily, printed in New Bedford, is published here upon the ground.

With regard to the clergy, there are twelve different Methodist Conferences represented here by one or more ministers each, — some by large numbers, of course, — not as appointed delegates, but voluntary visitors. They have heard and read of the Martha's Vineyard Camp-meeting, and have come to see the veritable lion. So of large numbers of laymen.

The petition to the Legislature for an act of incorporation, ordered last year, having, for some reason, failed of success, it had been voted, at one of the sessions of the Association this year, to renew the request; and a new Committee was appointed. They were Hon. George F. Gavitt, William Mason, Esq., and Hon. Robert C. Pitman.

In a meeting of the Association this morning, a vote was passed, instructing the Committee appointed to procure incorporation, to ask for power to hold property in an amount not exceeding seventy-five thousand dollars. It was designed to ask that what was strictly the property of the Association might be exempted from taxation, the same as our houses of worship at our homes were.

Up to two o'clock to-day, five hundred and seventy tent and cottage lots had been licensed for the year. A meeting of cottage and tent owners was held at one o'clock, to take into consideration the subject of building a substantial fence between the grounds of the Camp-meeting Association and lands of other parties adjoining. A proposition to build such a fence was voted down.

The sermon of the forenoon was by Rev. William Livesey, of Middletown, R. I.; and in the afternoon, by Rev. T. Willard Lewis, of Charleston, S. C. Rev. Mr. Conant, of Millville, preached in the evening, and was followed in an address from Rev. Charles Munger, of Maine.

Sabbath. At eight o'clock we were called together for the accustomed Camp-meeting Love Feast. Some thousands assembled. Rev. William Livesey opened the service, and presided. The invitation was given to the members of other churches to participate freely in the speaking, and a very considerable number of such availed themselves of the privilege accorded to them. Among these was a gentleman who said he was "a Presbyterian, sixteen hundred miles from home." Many persons spoke of this as their spiritual birthplace in years past, and others gave testimony as to the blessings here experienced, and the number of years they had been in attendance here. It was a time of great spiritual animation and holy joy. To appreciate duly, however, one must be present at a scene of the kind.

The preaching in the forenoon was by Rev. David H. Ela, of Trinity Church, Providence. At one o'clock was a gathering of the children at the stand. Rev. Mr. Bates presided. Short addresses were given, and Mr. Phillips furnished the music. Mr. P.'s performances, on this and other occasions at this meeting, were of that purely religious character, both as to the sentiments of his pieces and the style of performing them, that he beautifully harmonized with both ministry and laity in their efforts to do good.

The afternoon sermon was by Rev. S. D. Brown, of the New York Bedford Street Church. It was a production marked by much ability and an excellent spirit.

Besides the three or four steamers daily plying between New Bedford and other neighboring places and this populous location, all of which came with large crowds of people, a boat came from Providence, and another from New York. There were believed to be in and about the grounds, at midday, some ten or twelve thousand, including the regular campers, and those temporarily here. Besides steamers, packets, sail-boats, carriages, all available means of conveyance are put in requisition on the camp-meeting Sabbath, if the day be favorable, as this was. The congregation at the stand, although large, was not so large as in some previous years, owing to the want of shade over many of the seats. This lack it was designed to remedy the next year by means of awnings.

The School Ship was anchored in the harbor near us. Among those who came on her, and who paid a visit to the ground, was the Hon. F. B. Sanborn, of Concord, Mass., Secretary of the Massachusetts Board of State Charities, and James Redpath, Esq.

The sanctity of the Sabbath was observed in several things, if not in all. The row boats which were let on week days were anchored off away from the piers, and the stores and other places of business suspended operation, excepting so far as was required for the supply of the necessary food. The carriage drivers also had to suspend operations. Having occasion to go to the new wharf, when the steamers for New Bedford left at half past four o'clock, human beings appeared in clouds. Two steamers left loaded, carrying about two thousand people, and still the wharf and bluffs were thronged. Passing into the grounds, we found still other thousands. Although great multitudes left, the evening audience was the largest of the day. People could then be comfortable in the seats. The thousands assembled listened to Rev. Ira G. Bidwell, of Chestnut Street Church, Providence.

There was deep feeling in the audience. Many ministers and brethren entered earnestly into the work of the prayer-meeting which followed the sermon. A few persons professed conversion at the time.

On Monday the masses that had been moving campward within the last few days were now moving homeward. Still there were respectable numbers left. Rev. Henry D. Robinson, of Taunton, preached in the forenoon. Father Tillinghast held his accustomed children's meeting at one o'clock, and Rev. J. D. King, of Fall River First Church, preached the last sermon at the afternoon hour. At the closing service in the evening, there were several addresses, singing, and prayer, as usual on such occasions of late years. Thus closed the religious exercises of the thirty-second camp-meeting held in this consecrated grove.

At one of the business sessions, S. P. Coffin, Esq., was rechosen Agent, and Jeremiah Pease, Esq., Treasurer. The Finance Committee had also been elected. At different sessions of the Association, the following items were passed. J. C. Brock, S. Reed, and W. B. Lawton were appointed a Committee to revise the Rules of the Camp-meeting.

In addition to the provisions previously made for membership, there was added, as an amendment, "And such other persons as the Association shall elect by a two thirds vote of members present, and voting." And thereupon Rev. George W. Stearns, Dr. Moses L. Scudder, and Rev. John H. Twombly were elected members.

The Finance Committee were authorized to provide ways and means to defray the expenses of obtaining the act of incorporation to be asked for.

The same Committee were instructed to provide suitable accommodations for ministerial brethren from abroad. One of the resolutions was as follows: —

"*Resolved*, That it is contrary to the established policy of the Martha's Vineyard Camp-meeting Association for any one person to hold for occupancy for himself, or for hire, more than one cottage or tent lot upon said camp-meeting premises, with the exception of such lots as are used for culinary purposes in the rear of such cottages or tents, or when such lots are leased for the erection of double buildings thereon."

In one of its enactments the Association declared that the design of holding an annual camp-meeting at Martha's Vineyard was strictly religious, and that this design should be paramount to all others; also, that the security, simplicity, and moral integrity of the social and domestic life that have hitherto attended this camp-meeting have arisen from the distinctive religious influence that has characterized it.

A Committee was appointed to consider what means can be used to insure the efficiency of the M. V. Camp-meeting. It consisted of Rev. Lewis B. Bates, Rev. Frederick Upham, D. D., Rev. James D. Butler, Hon. William B. Lawton, Rev. John H. Twombly, and Messrs. Noah Tripp, John D. Flint, and Pardon M. Stone. The Presiding Elder of the Providence District to be, *ex officio*, Chairman.

CHAPTER XI.

CAMP-MEETING OF 1868.

SOME days before the commencement of this camp-meeting the author had occasion to note facts of interest. It may seem like repeating an old story to say, that of the numbers present so long before the meeting, the doings, and the surroundings, there never had been the like seen in any former year. The fact is, this is emphatically an institution of progress. The rustication, the coming and going of people, and the pastimes, were all on a larger scale than ever before. Pleasant days passed; quiet reigned; religious influence, as usual, was dominant. There were public prayers at eight o'clock A. M. at the ringing of the bell, prayer-meetings every evening, and preaching every Sabbath. About forty-five new cottages had risen here this season as by magic; and the hammers, saws, planes, and paint-brushes were still being plied from early morn till dewy eve. It was one of the most business-like places on the island. One of the builders — Mr. Charles Worth — had been employed here nearly the entire year. Work was to be suspended, of course, during camp-meeting days, to be resumed afterward. Some few of the cottages had been constructed with French roofs, thus giving more room in the attics. The cost of such was from twelve hundred dollars to fifteen hundred dollars; average cost of cottages, six hundred dollars. Many of the cottage and tent doors were open, displaying a cosy interior and quietly busy occupants, sewing, reading, &c.

To the list of excellent boarding-houses and boarding-tents was added, this year, the "Narragansett House." We were supplied with a market and a sales depot of a New Bedford bakery. There were a hardware store and lumber yard, kept by Mr. Edwin R. Coffin, of Edgartown. He had sold here this season two hundred thousand feet of lumber. Matthew P. Butler, Esq., of Tisbury, and Brock & Gifford, of New Bedford, had stores, in which were kept a great variety of needful articles. There were other places of the kind of less note. Richard G. Shute and Enoch C. Cornell, artists, were established in nice cottages, doing their accustomed business. Others of the same craft were expected here, as usual. The entire property on the grounds of the Camp-meeting Association, including the grounds themselves, was estimated at two hundred thousand dollars. The most of this, of course, belonged to the many hundreds of private individuals.

On the grounds of the Oak Bluffs Land and Wharf Company several nice cottages had been built, and also a house of entertainment, called the "Oak Bluffs House." Of late about fifty lots, at one hundred dollars each, had been taken on that side. The company had shown great enterprise. They had added eighty feet in length to their wharf, making it three hundred and twenty feet long. This wharf was very substantial. The ice of the long winter made no impression upon it. Its whole cost had been six thousand dollars. The land and buildings of the company, including the seatings on the bluffs to accommodate visitors, had cost eight thousand five hundred dollars. The company were taxed for fifteen thousand dollars.

August 24. This was the day for commencing the meeting. Three thousand people had come before. The name of "camp-meeting," as applied to this great gathering, was no misnomer, notwithstanding the changed aspects. "The Israelites dwelt in tents;" so do most of us here. But why should more substantial houses be thought inconsistent with the sanctities of the place? Some characterize our gathering as a "picnic." It is nothing of the kind. Some do, indeed, rusticate here during their summer respite; and may they not do so here as well as anywhere? But on the camp-meeting days we have a camp-meeting still. Some ask, "What is this place going to be?" Answer: "The same that it is now, only more of it." How much the increase was to be, none could foresee.

On the Sabbath preceding the beginning, there were sermons by Rev. Samuel C. Brown, Presiding Elder of the Providence District, Rev. William E. Stanton, Pastor of the First Baptist Church in Lowell, and Rev. S. F. Upham, of the Hanover Street Church in Boston.

As an indication of the general religious influence which seemed to pervade the place and inspire reverence in all minds, before the camp-meeting proper, I give a statement made to me the day before the meeting by a Baptist clergyman who had been stopping on the grounds for more than a week. He said that during that time he had not heard a profane word from any one, nor even a slang word.

It was remarked by one a few days before the meeting that this was a camp-meeting of weeks, with one week of special services. Perhaps this may not be strictly true; but certain it is that the transition from the preceding weeks to the one of the meeting proper was so simple and easy, that, but for the character and increased frequency of the public religious services and the increased number of people, we should hardly know when the change took place.

In a great institution there is very much to be done that may be properly denominated outside work. It is emphatically the case with this. There is the laying out of the grounds into parks, avenues, and lots; the assignment of tent and cottage lots to the numerous applicants; the issuing of licenses, or leases of these lots; clearing up every season extensive grounds of the underbrush, and the whole encampment of accumulated leaves and litter; the making of new roads and other arrangements to accommodate travel to and from the grounds, and the removing from one position to another of large boarding establishments and stores, to answer the increasing demands for cottage and tent lots; the purchasing of tons of straw, and selling out the same at retail; the providing of the means of lighting this extensive encampment; making the needful arrangements for transportation on steamboats and railroads at reduced fares for the occasion; and last, but not least, providing means to meet the large expenses accruing in these operations: these are some of the things to be done. This year, among other improvements, the road which once was the main entrance to the ground from the west, was closed as such, and laid out as an avenue, called Clinton Avenue, on which ranges of beautiful cottages were erected on each side of its broad space. A road was made, instead, along by the pond shore, coming in by the lumber yard.

On the evening of the 24th the first public service of the camp-meeting was held at the stand. As the custom had been of late years, instead of a sermon there were several addresses from clergymen. The exercises were impressive, and indicative of good to come. On the successive days of the meeting, the details were quite similar to those of other gatherings of the kind. At ten o'clock of the 25th the preaching was by Rev. John Allen, of Maine. The sermon of the afternoon was by Rev. J. H. James, of Warren, R. I. The evening audience was large, the air still, and the words of the preacher — Rev. Varnum A. Cooper — could be heard at quite a distance. The sentiments of the text, which were cogently urged, were a sermon of themselves.

26th. As had been the case in successive years, a large portion of the crowds of people who continue to come from day to day were strangers to us, who had been attendants here for so many years. To be sure, we see many familiar faces, but very few, indeed, of those who greeted us in the first years of the encampment. "The fathers — where are they?" was a question which might be asked with a great deal of emphasis. We who had always been here felt their absence as none others could. Most of those old Christian warriors had gone to join the army above.

The friends from Edgartown to-day were saddened by the intelligence that the venerable Thomas M. Coffin, father of Sirson P. Coffin, the efficient Agent of this Camp-meeting Association, went to his heavenly rest at two o'clock this morning. Mr. Coffin was one of the early strong men of the Methodist church in Edgartown, and has always remained one of its pillars. He was a man of unblemished moral character, true to the church of his choice, giving liberally of his means for the support of the gospel. He joined the church in 1812, and was, when he died, about eighty-eight years of age. "His end was peace," but the church mourns. Mr. Coffin was among the number who first selected, in this then wilderness, the spot for the "Preachers' Stand." He was one of the first to lease this grove for the purposes of a camp-meeting, and had charge of one of the first of the Edgartown society tents on this ground. It is therefore fitting that in this connection we should pay this brief tribute to his memory.

One of the most interesting facts connected with our gathering in this grove is, the free commingling of people of different religious denominations. All make themselves at home in their quiet domiciles. The preaching is of course mainly by Methodist ministers, but others occasionally participate. Prominent laymen, as well as prominent ministers, are here from different States. Among the former are the Hon. Sylvander Johnson, of North Adams, one of the State Directors of the Western Railroad, and Warren Ladd, Esq., Superintendent of the railroads terminating in New Bedford and Fairhaven. Among the clergymen was Rev. Dr. William Butler, late missionary to India.

Of steamboats we had a *quantum sufficit* for the accommodation of all travellers to and from the landings. Added to the three in the interest of the steamboat company, was the steamer Emeline, of Boston, put on as an opposition boat.

The sermons of the day were by Rev. S. A. Winsor, of East Greenwich, R. I., Rev. F. J.

Wagner, of St. Paul's Church, Fall River, and Dr. F. Upham, of Fairhaven.

August 27. Each day at such an assemblage brings with it its work. Fresh themes, new points of interest, new views, new thoughts, new facts, and new combinations involving new duties, are continually being developed.

The sermon of the forenoon was by Rev. Mr. Angier, of the Congregational Church at Edgartown. Text, 2 Chron. xv. 7 : " Be strong, therefore." Principal theme, "The Sources of Strength." Both the structure of the sermon, and the spirit in which it was delivered, were highly approved.

The sermon of the afternoon was by Rev. A. W. Paige, of Stoughton, on " Heart Religion."

During the afternoon of this day there was a meeting of ladies in the Warren, R. I., tent, to consider maternal duties. It was addressed by Mrs. Dr. Butler, late of the India mission, in a manner which thrilled the hearts of those present. There were also meetings in the Edgartown tent, addressed by Mrs. Langford, sister of the celebrated Mrs. Dr. Palmer, and by Mrs. Wright, widow of the late Minister Wright, who died at Berlin about a year and a half previous. The subject on which these two dwelt was that of Christian holiness. The last named lady was especially instructive.

The opening prayer of the evening service was by the Rev. Dr. A. H. Quint, Congregationalist, of New Bedford, and the sermon which followed was by the Rev. L. B. Bates, of the same city. The wind, some part of the day, was very high, so much so that the steamer had to land at the wharf west of the Chop.

Friday, 28th. The air was still salubrious, and prayer and praise in rich profusion greeted the ear. It had been decided to hold two Love Feasts during this encampment, the first of which was appointed for this morning. Large numbers assembled. Rev. Dr. Upham presided, and the opening prayer was offered by the Rev. Paul Townsend, of Mansfield. The largest liberty was given to Christians of all names, and quite a number of both ministers and laymen of other churches freely participated. A very large number of persons gave testimony, among whom were Mrs. Langford and Mrs. Wright, before noticed.

The preaching at ten o'clock was by Rev. James A. Dean, and at two o'clock by Rev. Edward H. Hatfield. The preacher of the evening was Dr. William Butler, late missionary to India. Seventeen years previous, before he went on his Eastern mission, he preached here to great acceptance. The studies, experiences, and labors of those years had not been lost upon him. He showed that he was still more the man of power.

Saturday, 29th. Altogether this is a wonderful place. Its original adaptedness as a place for holding camp-meetings, its primitive oaks, its bold waters and sightly bluffs, its pleasant walks and invigorating atmosphere, its facilities for the preservation of good order, the long continuance of occupancy, its increased conveniences for visitors, the increase of numbers in attendance, and especially its history as a place where great good has been done, — all unite to render it a place of great interest and of pleasant resort. Intrinsically excellent as the scenery has been in by-gone years, the beautiful cottages are not the only addition to its charms. The improvements at "Oak Bluffs" are not only useful, but highly ornamental to the place. The substantial dock, the buildings on the bluffs, the fields adorned with green, the coming and going of steamers, the bluffs at such times being lined with spectators for a long distance, aid in forming a delightful picture. Besides the frequent arrivals and departures of steamers, the waters are visited by numerous yachts, of which there seems to be a greater abundance than ever this year. The noble School Ship is also riding at anchor near by. As the meeting is culminating in interest, increased crowds come down upon the steamers. Very many, however, come merely for the excursion, and return either on the same or the following day.

The sermon of the forenoon was by Rev. A. N. Bodfish, of Newport, R. I., that of the afternoon by Rev. D. A. Wheeden, of Bristol, R. I., and that of the evening by Rev. A. J. Church, of Edgartown. Friend Tillinghast had a throng of children present in the Pleasant Street tent in the morning. After the preaching in the afternoon, the sacrament of the Lord's Supper was administered to about forty ministers and to large numbers of the laity. The sermon of the evening, by Mr. Church, on the worth of the soul, and kindred subjects, seemed deeply to impress the concourse of people assembled to hear.

Sabbath, August 30. The second Love Feast was held this morning, at eight o'clock, conducted by Rev. A. D. Sargeant, of the New England Conference. It was a very large gathering — so large that it was not easy to confine the speaking to one at a time, and frequently several would be upon their feet at the same moment. The testimonies, as was recommended, were very short, and in less than an hour and a half two hundred and thirty persons spoke — the singing of a verse or two frequently intervening between speeches. Persons of different denominations, as on the former occasion, were invited to give testimony; and several did, and among them the Hon. Amasa Walker, of Brookfield, formerly Secretary of this Commonwealth. He spoke cordially of the camp-meeting and its objects, and urged the continuance of these meetings as a means of grace. He never was here before, but liked the place and the spirit manifested here. The Methodist denomination was doing a great work. He thought his own denomination (Congregational) would imitate us in the holding of camp-meetings.

There were noticed in the audience Senator Sprague, of Rhode Island, and other persons of distinction. The sermon of the forenoon was by Rev. Charles H. Payne, formerly of this Conference, then pastor of a church in Philadelphia. While some five thousand people were listening to this speaker, there was preaching in two other places; viz., in Forest Circle by Rev. Mr. Patterson, and in Fourth Street Avenue by Rev. Mr. Pressberry. At one o'clock the children's meeting was addressed by Senator Sprague, the singing being by yachtmen. At two o'clock the multitude were again assembled. Rev. Dr. Tiffany, of New Brunswick, N. J., was the preacher introduced. His text was Isaiah xlv., last clause of twenty-third verse. The sermon was rich in thought, eloquent in words, and a model in the style of delivery. About six thousand people were within the circle to hear, and other thousands would probably have been better employed than they were, had they been there too.

It was estimated that about four thousand

people were permanently stopping upon the grounds; that from fifteen to twenty thousand different persons were at the place during two weeks; and that more than one hundred clergymen of different denominations, mostly Methodists, were present during the whole or some part of the meeting.

Four steamboats and several sailing vessels had left after the afternoon service, bearing away their precious freights of human beings of both sexes and of various ages and positions in life, to the number of about five thousand. Others left by conveyances of less magnitude. Still the audience of the evening was not more than a thousand or two less than in the daytime. Before night, a cloud rising in the distance threatened a shower of rain; but as it seemed held in abeyance, the people crowded to the seats to listen again to the word of the Lord.

It was intimated that the last sermon of the day was to be by Rev. George Lansing Taylor, of Brooklyn, New York. This proved to be true. He took his text in Judges, chapter vii., the last part of verse 20 — "The Sword of the Lord and of Gideon." Two elements enter into the composition of whatever blesses man, and these combine. To realize any real benefit, God and man must unite. If we want any good, God must be in it. Israel had done wrong, and, as a legitimate consequence, was brought into trouble. Inimical neighboring nations came in upon them, and swept over their land. They were in a sad condition. They cried unto God, and he heard them. He always hears us when we cry unto him. The preacher proceeded to describe, in his remarkably graphic style, the deliverance of the Israelites, the means by which it was accomplished, the manner of its accomplishment, and the consequences, using the facts as given in the history of the matter to illustrate the Christian labor, warfare, and experience. The call of Gideon, the tests used on the part of God, and those desired by Gideon himself to substantiate and authenticate his divine call to the work, were delineated and applied, not only with characteristic energy, but also with a real zest. Then the depleting of the army of thirty-two thousand, till but three hundred men were left, to show that the deliverance was of God, and not of man, afforded other practical reflections.

About this time the shower of rain came gently, and some began to leave the seats. The preacher exhorted them to remain and hear, and, the rain holding up, the majority became quiet for a while. But presently it rained again, and the meeting was adjourned to the large County Street tent. The tent being crowded, and large numbers gathering near each entrance, the preacher proceeded. At the same time prayer-meetings were entered upon in several of the large tents to accommodate the masses who could gain no admittance to the place of preaching. Before he concluded, the preacher rather facetiously said that the two swords — the "sword of the Lord" and the "sword of Gideon," both of which were used — were, when placed back to back, a two-edged sword, like the sword of the truth of God, which cuts both ways.

The effect of the sermon was electrical upon both saint and sinner, and at its close more than twenty persons were induced to present themselves for prayers. One man, who had been so indifferent that he had remained in the tent, and would not go out to the service at the stand, when the meeting came to him was so affected by the word spoken, that he bowed with the others in humble supplication, and ere the close of the service sensibly felt that his sins had been pardoned.

Monday morning came. The rain had cooled the atmosphere, and the cheerful sun, with his kindly rays, again beamed in upon us through the leafy canopy. Many were leaving in the early boats. It was the last day of the meeting. A comparatively small audience assembled at the hour of ten A. M. Rev. David H. Ela, of Providence, preached. The sermon of the afternoon was by Rev. Samuel F. Upham, of Boston. The closing service at the evening hour was in the accustomed form — singing, prayer, addresses by the President of the meeting and others. Following this was the old-fashioned closing ceremony revived. It consisted in marching around the circle, singing, and then all shaking hands with every minister and with every other person who was pleased to join in the marching column.

In reviewing the business matters passed upon by the Association at its sessions during this camp-meeting, we find items of interest. The Committee appointed last year to renew application to the State Legislature for an act of incorporation, having been successful in their efforts, reported through their chairman, Hon. George F. Gavitt. The report of the Committee was accepted, and the charter itself accepted and adopted. The President and Secretary of last year were rechosen, *pro tem.*, and a set of bylaws for the government of the Corporation presented and adopted. One of these by-laws provides for a Board of Directors of eighteen persons, six of whom were to be ministers, and twelve of whom were to be laymen. Six of the board — two ministers and four laymen — were to serve three years, six two years, and six one year; thus making six elective each year to fill the places of the outgoing six. At a subsequent meeting, officers for the year were chosen as follows: President, Rev. Samuel C. Brown, D. D.; Clerk, Rev. David H. Ela; Treasurer, Jeremiah Pease, Esq.*

The playing of croquet on these grounds hav-

* See Appendix for List of Officers and Board of Directors entire.

ing become very fashionable of late years by those rusticating here previously to the commencement of the camp-meeting services, the following resolution, passed at one of the sessions, is understood to have reference to this practice within the circle of the large tents.

"*Resolved*, That the grounds, seats, and stand, and society tents, within the large circle, for the entire year, be only used as they are during the time of camp-meeting, and the Directors are requested by the Association to see that this resolution is carried out."

Near the close of this camp-meeting it was stated that, in addition to the extensive grounds previously acquired by the Association, an additional purchase of fifty-five acres had been negotiated with Tarlton C. Luce, Esq., by parties connected with our Corporation. This tract lies north-westerly from the central part of the camp ground, and consists of both wood and cleared land. It seems, however, that the purchase was not fully matured, and that its consummation rested upon certain conditions not fully acceded to.

The following letter was written by a professional gentleman of high respectability in the city of Brooklyn, N. Y., who was stopping here, two days before the commencement of this camp-meeting : —

> MARTHA'S VINEYARD CAMP GROUND,
> August 22, 1868.

"This is one of the most delightful spots on earth to go for a summer's vacation. The camp-meeting ground, or Wesleyan Grove, as it is called, is situated in the township of Edgartown, on the Island of Martha's Vineyard, in the State of Massachusetts, about three miles from the town of Holmes Hole,* and seven miles from Edgartown. It is but a few hundred yards from the steamboat landing, which makes it convenient for visitors to reach. The walk from the landing to the ground is delightful, and the scenery romantic. As we rise a small hill, we behold the deep blue sea, with here and there a sail on our left, and a beautiful shady grove before, through which we are to pass in order to reach the camp ground. The soil is sandy, and absorbs the rain about as fast as it falls; we are, therefore, even in wet weather, free from mud. This is a great desideratum to those

---

* Holmes Hole forms a part of the town of Tisbury.

who spend the summer months in this delightful grove. The Martha's Vineyard Camp Ground' was selected by the late Jeremiah Pease, of Edgartown, and the first meeting was held on Monday, the 24th day of August, 1835, at which only nine tents graced the circle. A meeting has been held on the ground every year since, except in 1845.

"The camp ground at the Vineyard is perhaps about three times the size of Fort Greene, or rather Washington Park, of your city. The grove is composed of venerable oaks of many years' standing, and is beautifully laid out in parks, avenues, and streets. We have Trinity Park, Central Park, County Park, Forest Circle, Grand Circle, &c. Then we have Broadway, Cottage Avenue, Lake Avenue, Narragansett Avenue, Fisk Avenue, Rock Avenue, Washington Avenue, Clinton Avenue, Allen Street Avenue, Commonwealth Avenue, Fourth Street Avenue. We also have Montgomery Place, Scott Place, Upham's Hill, County Street, Sunnyside, Mount Pleasant, and a host of others. These parks and streets are neatly laid out, and are surrounded with cottages, tents, and cottage tents; the latter being composed of boards and sail-cloth. There are now about two hundred cottages on the ground, and eight hundred tents and cottage tents, making about ten hundred in all. Over forty of the cottages on the camp ground have been erected during the past year, and four of the number, built on Clinton Avenue, are owned by citizens of Brooklyn, viz., John Q. Maynard, John French, Rev. C. H. Payne, and Dr. D. E. Smith. The avenue is over seventy feet wide, and these buildings are pronounced by strangers to be the neatest and best arranged cottages on the ground. They are magnificently furnished, and are certainly very convenient in many particulars. These gentlemen, with their families, have been spending the past six weeks in their new homes.

"The parks, streets, and avenues are lighted with petroleum oil lamps holding one quart each, and placed about one hundred feet apart. The lamp posts are wood, turned, painted, and sanded. The lanterns are in size and form similar to those in the streets of Brooklyn. These lamps, when lighted, are a magnificent sight, and must be seen to be fully realized.

"The Martha's Vineyard Camp Ground may truly be called a city in the woods — a religious watering-place on a huge scale, as nearly every State in the Union is here represented. The majority of the cottages are inhabited during the months of June, July, and August, and many families remain until October. The following programme will give you an idea of what we do daily at the Vineyard. The gong sounds precisely at half past six A. M. We have breakfast at seven; morning prayer at eight, in a huge tent seating about one thousand persons; bathe at nine; dine at twelve M.; go sailing, fishing, blueberrying, or rambling on the beach for shells or odd stones in the afternoon; tea, six P. M.; preaching, or prayer-meeting, or experience meeting every evening. On Sundays we have three sermons from different preachers, who are stopping on the ground. These meetings are only preliminary to the grand finale, which will commence on Monday, the 24th of August, and continue until the 2d day of September.

"We have excellent fishing, delightful bathing, splendid sailing, and the pure, invigorating breezes from the ocean. We have boarding-houses that will accommodate from five to eight hundred persons, and good substantial board at from seven to ten dollars per week; and if there is a spot on God's green earth where a man may take solid comfort, it is at the Martha's Vineyard Camp Ground.

"M. D."

CHAPTER XII.

CAMP-MEETING OF 1869.

THIS meeting, like that of last year, was preceded by extensive building and a long season of rustication. Both, indeed, have been on a much larger scale than in any previous year. Altogether, on the Association's grounds and on the Oak Bluffs side, there have been built nearly one hundred cottages, some of them very nice, with French roofs. The most expensive on the Oak Bluffs is the new cottage of E. P. Carpenter, Esq., of Foxboro', and on the camp ground that of Senator Sprague, of Rhode Island, which has been put up at a cost of some thirty-five hundred dollars. It is very richly furnished. There have also been erected several large stores; several houses of entertainment — one or two of them on the European plan. Other places of business have been established, including a market, built in a novel style. Some of the workmen have been busy here nearly the entire year. But while individual enterprise has been manifest on a large scale, the camp-meeting Directors have not been idle. An ice-house has been built, which promises to be a source of revenue in years to come. They have also erected a high picket-fence all around the camp ground proper, including some acres, recently purchased, adjoining the original premises on the south-west. The passage in and out is by gateways. It is held that this fence will be a great help in the enforcement of police regulations, and a means of protection to the property on the camp ground limits.

A temporary awning was extended over a very considerable portion of the seating at the stand, which, on account of the depleted state of the foliage, afforded a very desirable protection on sunny days and in moderately wet weather. This supplied, in part, a desideratum, and it is hoped it will be succeeded by something of the kind which will be permanent and more complete. It would add thousands to the congregations at the public services. Even the limited and quite imperfect awning of this year has secured better congregations at the day preaching services than have been in attendance for several years last past.

Great numbers of people came to the place during the summer, some merely on an excursion, or for a day or two, others to rusticate for their summer vacation. Before the time of the camp-meeting proper, thousands were here. The usual recreations and pastimes were enjoyed. Walking, berrying, fishing, boating, swinging, and croqueting, — especially the last-named, — were participated in, not only by children and youth, but by large numbers of children of a larger growth, some of them gray-headed children. Even some ministers were as earnestly engaged in the game of croquet as any of the juveniles. This last exercise held on up to the day of the meeting, and the last few hours were as energetically improved as though all of earthly bliss depended on the improvement of the remaining hours. But when the time came, the whole was as thoroughly abandoned. While the pure, invigorating air was inhaled, and the rustic exercises were improved both for health and pastime, religious duties were not lost sight of. Some of the principal visitors were religious men, and, as usual, in these weeks of vacation, frequent religious meetings were held — prayer-meetings and occasional preaching in the week time, and preaching on the Sabbath. For several weeks the Rev. A. J. Church, of Edgartown, went regularly on Wednesday, and preached, in the evening, to the workmen and such others as chose to hear. Then others preached occasionally. During the last two weeks preceding the meeting, there was almost always a supply of preachers on the ground; and the prayer-meetings and morning prayers, under the direction of John Allen, Esq., of Newport, were like the preparation days among the Israelites. They were the crimson light dawning in upon the camp, heralding the great feast of the soul remaining in store.

One of the tarrying days was enlivened by a marriage at the stand. The parties were from Woonsocket, R. I. A large concourse of people — from fifteen hundred to two thousand — were present to witness the ceremonies, which were conducted according to book, Rev. J. W.

Willet officiating, with the exception of the legalizing of the banns, which was performed by Sirson P. Coffin, Esq.

On Saturday evening preceding the commencement of the camp-meeting, there was a grand illumination, accompanied with fireworks, on Oak Bluffs. Music was furnished by the Foxboro' Brass Band. But notwithstanding this entertainment, which called out its thousands to witness it, there were, at the same time, two largely-attended prayer-meetings in the camp. And such was the Christian influence here, and such the general good character of the thousands on both sides of the line, that on Monday evening, August 16, the day of the commencement of the camp-meeting proper, and thenceforward through the week, all these recreating scenes were as quiet as on a Sabbath.

The Sabbath preceding the beginning was one of great interest. The preaching in the forenoon was by Rev. John E. Searles, of Brooklyn, N. Y., and in the afternoon by Rev. William Butler, D. D., the late founder, under circumstances of great peril, of the Methodist mission in India. He now represented, as an agent, the American and Foreign Christian Union, and took a collection for that cause, amounting to one hundred and fourteen dollars and eleven cents.

Among the distinguished visitors to the ground within a week or two of the time of the meeting, were Rev. Dr. Cummings, President of the Wesleyan University at Middletown, Conn., the venerable Rev. Edward T. Taylor, for very many years preacher at the Seaman's Bethel, Boston, and the Hon. Josiah Quincy, also of Boston; also the Hon. Charles L. Flint, Secretary of the State Board of Agriculture. There had been, during the season, several excursions of Sabbath Schools to these grounds, among these one in which the Sabbath Schools of all the churches of the different denominations on the island were invited to participate.

On Saturday, the 14th, there was held in the large Matthewson Street tent, a meeting of the Ladies' Missionary Society of the Methodist Episcopal Church, formed some months previous, of which society Mrs. Dr. Butler was President, and Mrs. Rev. J. H. Twombly was Secretary. The meeting was addressed by the

President, and by Mrs. Wright, widow of the late Governor Wright, who died while American Minister at the Court of Berlin. The society held several other meetings during the following days of the camp-meeting.

The service introductory to the series of the camp-meeting week was held at the stand, as appointed, on Monday evening, August 16. On account of the dampness and chilliness of the evening, the exercises were quite brief. They were conducted by Rev. Samuel C. Brown, D. D., Superintendent of the camp-meeting. Appropriate remarks were made by him, and also by Rev. J. D. King, of Fall River, and Rev. John Allen, of Maine.

Tuesday. The sermon of the forenoon was by Rev. Edwin D. Hall, of Pawtucket, R. I. The afternoon being unfavorable for preaching at the stand, there were services at four of the large tents, led by Rev. F. Upham, D. D., Rev. D. A. Whedon, D. D., Rev. John Allen, of Maine, and Rev. J. W. Willet, of Rockville, Conn.

The sermon of the evening was by Rev. John P. Newman, D. D., of the new Washington Metropolitan Church, and Chaplain of the

United States Senate. A large congregation were assembled at the stand. The text was John iii. 11: "Verily, verily, I say unto thee, We speak that we do know, and testify that we have seen; and ye receive not our witness." The leading thought of the sermon was the importance of personal experience. The mass of the people cannot contend successfully with the cavils of infidels like Hume and Voltaire, and others, but they can tell what they feel and know, which is a stronger argument than any mere deduction of the intellect. Some people object to experimental religion because all are not converted alike, arguing thus against its validity on account of its want of unity in those who profess it. But religion does not profess to change the peculiar personal traits of a man's constitution. You would not expect a man of a naturally cheerful disposition to put on at conversion an air of gloom and melancholy, nor *vice versa*. What a man is he will be in his natural disposition. There is a great diversity also in Christian experience, this experience being shaped in its manifestations by the peculiar natural traits of the individual. It is all one thing, only it takes on different shapes. Matter is in various forms, and with various simple elements, yet it is all matter. Take a prism and hold it up to the light, and it will resolve the light into different colors. Yet when, by the use of another prism, those rays are brought together again, they make a unit. So religious experience is a unit, although there is diversity in it. To what is the power of the Methodist church indebted? Not to her splendid churches nor her learned ministry, nor her numbers, nor her peculiar institutions, but to the personal experience of her members. The great object here is to know Jesus. And the great inquiry of the saved in heaven will be to see Jesus. It is a morbid idea to dwell upon as the chief source of pleasure in heaven that we shall see our friends there. The greatest of all will be to see Jesus.

Mrs. Wright, before named, commenced her meetings again in the Holmes Hole tent, at which Christian holiness was the theme. Dr. Newman occupied much of the time. The "Campmeeting Herald" made its appearance again in a daily issue, published by Lieut. Charles M. Vincent, editor of the "Vineyard Gazette."

Wednesday. The sermons of the day were by Rev. Charles H. Titus, of Warren, R. I., Rev. Joel E. Hawkins, of New Bedford Pleasant Street Church, and Rev. Varnum A. Cooper, of Providence, R. I. — earnest sermons, followed by exhortations and prayers. The ministers engaged in the work with a readiness and heartiness which gave promise of good results at this camp-meeting. The spirit of the meeting was excellent.

At the meeting of the Camp-meeting Association, on Tuesday, officers were chosen for the ensuing year. President, Rev. Samuel C. Brown, D. D.; Secretary, Rev. George L. Westgate; Treasurer, Jeremiah Pease, Esq. The six Directors elected for the year were the same that constituted the first class of last year, with the exception of Rev. L. B. Bates, who was chosen in place of Rev. D. H. Ela, who was transferred to the New England Conference last spring.

Some amendments were made in the by-laws, conforming them to the change in the districts as to membership, and recognizing the Presiding Elders of the three — Providence, New Bedford, and Sandwich. Also, all the Board of Directors, whether otherwise members or not, and the Treasurer and Agent, are to be, *ex officio*, members of the Association. The reports of the Board of Directors and of the Treasurer were submitted and accepted. A resolution was also passed tendering the cordial thanks of the Association to Jeremiah Pease, Esq., for his faithful services as Treasurer for the last eight years.

Thursday. Preaching by Rev. J. W. Willet, of Rockville, Ct., Rev. L. H. Angier, of Edgartown (Congregationalist), and Rev. Cyrus D. Foss, of New York. Persons came forward for prayers in considerable numbers.

Friday. Quite a number of conversions have occurred. The weather was favorable, with the exception of high winds, which made out-of-doors preaching rather laborious. The sermon of the forenoon was by Rev. J. D. King, of Fall River. At one o'clock there was a public prayer-meeting at the stand for the special purpose of praying for the divine blessing upon this camp-meeting. The sermon of the afternoon was by Rev. J. F. W. Barnes, of Providence, R. I. At six o'clock P. M., a meeting for the children under fourteen years of age was held in the Matthewson Street tent, and at the same hour a meeting for the young people above that age at the large County Street tent. The steamers brought great numbers. A vast assembly were gathered to hear the preaching of the evening, which was by Rev. J. O. Peck, of Worcester. The attention given to the preaching on this as on all other occasions, and the decorum manifest, were truly praiseworthy. Rev. S. F. Upham, of Boston Hanover Street Church, followed the preacher in an earnest exhortation, and in an invitation to those desiring prayers to come forward. Quite a number came.

Saturday. The day was warm. It had been announced that the Governor of the Commonwealth would come to the ground to-day. Between the hours of nine and ten A. M., the steamer Island Home arrived from Nantucket, bringing a large number of passengers, among them His Excellency, Governor William Claflin, accompanied by Hon. John Morissey, Sergeant at Arms. The Governor was the guest of Edmund Anthony, Esq., who had provided a cottage for his accommodation. Still, it was expected he would spend some time on board the School Ship Massachusetts, Captain Eldridge, anchored near. Although but little time intervened for attention to personal wants, His Excellency was promptly in attendance to hear the forenoon sermon, which was by Rev. L. B. Bates, of Taunton. Another general prayer-meeting was held at one o'clock, having the same object as the one at that hour the day previous.

It was reported that an accident had happened to the School Ship Barnard which was on her way hither with another company of distinguished persons, and that, in consequence, they would arrive late in the afternoon on the Revenue Cutter Vigilant, Captain Fengar. Colonel A. D. Hatch and Jeremiah Pease, Esq. had made arrangements for their accommodation on the ground, and in due time they arrived and were escorted to their quarters. They consisted of Judge Thomas Russell, Collector of Boston, and daughter, Hon. Henry Wilson, of the United States Senate, Hon. Benjamin F. Butler, of the United States House of Representatives, Ex-Senator Benjamin F. Wade and wife, and Mrs.

Hon. Oakes Ames. About the same time, Hon. William Sprague, United States Senator from Rhode Island, arrived, and took possession of his superb cottage, just built for him by Mr. Charles Worth. The sermon of the afternoon was by Rev. J. C. Sawyer, of the Providence Broadway Street Church. At six o'clock there was held a meeting of the Ladies' Missionary Society at the stand, at which Governor Claflin presided, and made a short address. . The evening was rainy, and preaching services were held in several of the large tents.

Sabbath. The rain had continued nearly the whole night, but in the morning the weather became more favorable, although the clouds still hung over us. By degrees they disappeared, and a good day ensued. The steamboats Monohansett, Canonicus, Helen Augusta, and Island Home, and other vessels had been busy, and vast numbers had come to see and hear. The many thousands in and about the grounds were expecting a day of great interest. The expectation of seeing and hearing men of eminence of course greatly heightened that interest.

At eight o'clock A. M. large numbers of

people assembled at the stand for the annual camp-meeting Love Feast. It was opened and conducted by Dr. F. Upham, who has been an effective Methodist minister nearly fifty years, and is to preach his semi-centennial at the Conference in the spring of 1870. One hundred and forty-five testimonies were given, interspersed with songs of praise. Ministry and laity, some of other denominations, but mostly our own, participated. Governor Sprague was present, and was an attentive listener. At the conclusion of the speaking, those who had not the time to speak as had others, were invited to give in their testimony by a show of hands, and a vast number gave the sign. Besides the regular service at the stand about to commence, preaching was announced by the Superintendent to take place at the same hour at several other places in the camp and vicinity. It occurred as follows: Entrance by Dunbar's, by Rev. A. J. Church; Cottage Avenue, by Rev. C. S. Rogers; Domestic Square, by Rev. J. W. F. Barnes; and on board School Ship Massachusetts, by Rev. L. B. Bates. Senator Wilson was one of the auditors of Rev. Mr. Church.

The sermon at the stand was by Rev. Micah J. Talbot, Presiding Elder of the New Bedford District. Governor Claflin was a hearer in the audience, declining to take a seat on the stand, to which he was urgently invited. The text was Isa. liii. 4, 5 : "Surely he hath borne our griefs and carried our sorrows; yet we did esteem him stricken, smitten of God, and afflicted. But he was wounded for our transgressions; he was bruised for our iniquities; the chastisement of our peace was upon him, and with his stripes we are healed." At one o'clock, as per assignment, by far the largest assembly was gathered at the stand for the Sabbath School celebration. The children were there in very considerable numbers in the front. Eager crowds hurried to the place before the time. The stand was crowded to a very uncomfortable degree. Ministers, laymen, a few ladies, who could, crowded up. It was judged there were ten thousand people assembled. Seats, altar, aisles, and the spaces outside the seats, were packed. There were, doubtless, far more standing than sitting. The Hutchinson family, who had been spending a day or two here, were present, by invitation, in the front part of the stand, to furnish their sweet music. Governor Claflin presided in his accustomed happy manner. After singing "Joy to the world," by the Hutchinsons, prayer was offered by Dr. Upham. Governor Claflin was then introduced as the President of the occasion, by Dr. Brown, the Superintendent of the camp-meeting. His Excellency proceeded to address those present. He congratulated them on the great advance which had been made in this department of usefulness since some of us were boys. We had not then the advantages we now have. He would by no means underrate the doings of those times. Perhaps we fail in some things. We children went then. Many go now who are older. We have much more now to attract to the Sabbath School. Much good has been done, but we look forward to the time when still greater achievements will be made. Christians must foster and cherish the Sabbath School. The common schools will not supply religious instruction; this must be done by the Sabbath School, under the labors of Christians. We must do this to save the nation. And what a delightful labor is that of the Sabbath School teacher! His reward is in heaven. We are informed by travellers in the old countries that the Coliseum of Rome, and other buildings, were just as they were described in the books they had read. So in the Book of Life with regard to the heaven it describes. He would not add more. Others were to follow. He would encourage all engaged in this work to labor on. He requested another song by the Hutchinson family. They sung "Climbing up Zion's hill."

The Governor then introduced Senator Henry Wilson. Mr. Wilson said the Christian men and women before him had assembled to devote a few moments to the Sabbath School cause. No institution in all the wide range of benevolent organizations is of more importance than the Sabbath School. That is to settle the fate of these United States. We believe in sustaining the interests of these United States, and we know they can only be sustained by the religion of Jesus Christ. We have moulded our institutions according to the Bible. That is the constitution of our country. We have had a great struggle in our country with a certain institution. That institution has gone down, no more to rise. Other things threaten us; ignorance and error — ignorance among ourselves and among the thousands from the Old World. We have got to enlighten them. Then, from the West, from Asia, they are coming in to meet us here in our continental empire. The training in the Sabbath School should be as extensive as that in the common school. He hoped the common schools would spread all down through the Southern portion of our vast domain, and that the Sabbath School would follow, and spread as widely.

On the conclusion of Mr. Wilson's address, the Governor requested another song, and the Hutchinsons favored us with the hymn of the " Millennium."

The Governor then disclaimed any disposition to confine the time of these addresses to laymen, and thought the clergymen, whose more particular business it was to instruct, should have a share. He introduced Rev. Dr. Moses L. Scudder, of Hartford, Conn. The doctor proceeded, in his usually terse style and energetic manner, to interest the vast audience. He alluded to the interest expressed for the country, but had no fears for its safety so long as we had such men as Governor Claflin and Senator Wilson to fill the positions they now do in the State and in the nation.

After the conclusion of Dr. Scudder's address and another song, the Governor said that when on board the School Ship, he asked the boys whom, of all the persons who addressed them, they liked best to hear; they immediately responded, "Judge Russell!" He introduced to the audience Judge Russell. The Judge proceeded in his happy manner to address, first, the children, counselling them to do right, — to begin right, — showing by many illustrations the importance of doing so. He then addressed the teachers, urging them on in their Christian work in that clear, perspicuous, and touching style for which he is eminent, and in which he carried the audience as by magic.

Another song. Mr. Turner, of the Hartford Asylum for the Deaf and Dumb, was present with a large company of deaf and dumb persons belonging on the island. He had been interpreting to them the addresses, and now gave, in sight of the audience, some specimens of his manner of teaching, and a prayer.

A vote of thanks was proposed by the Governor to the Hutchinsons for their excellent music on the occasion; and after once more singing, in which the whole congregation were invited to join, and did so, the meeting was dismissed, having been one of the most interesting occasions ever witnessed on this ground.

On account of the protracted exercises just noted, the preaching service of the afternoon was postponed to three o'clock. The preacher was Rev. D. A. Whedon, D. D., of Bristol, R. I. His text was John iii. 36 — " He that believeth on the Son hath everlasting life; and he that believeth not the Son shall not see life, but the wrath of God abideth on him." The one great theme of Scripture is salvation from sin. The one great condition of salvation is believing in the Lord Jesus Christ. There was preaching at the same hour at several other places. Near evening there was preaching at Oak Bluffs by Rev. L. B. Bates, for the eleventh year at or near the same place. At six o'clock there was another young people's meeting. About that time the Hutchinsons sung in Clinton Avenue.

Although thousands left in the steamers and

otherwise, there was a very large congregation in the evening. The preacher was the Rev. Alonzo Webster, D. D., of Charleston, S. C., and Presiding Elder of that District. He preached from Heb. x. 26 — "There remaineth no more sacrifice for sins." This was the last sermon of the series — the last of the present camp-meeting. It was followed by a powerful exhortation from Rev. Dr. Upham, who at the close of his address invited persons forward for prayers. A most interesting prayer-meeting followed. Twenty-five came forward. The meeting lasted till about eleven o'clock. At about every public preaching service at the stand, the sermon has been followed up in a similar way, and at nearly every such meeting not a few persons have professed conversion. The number converted during this camp-meeting is estimated variously from fifty to seventy. There has been no such meeting as this here for very many years. It is fully proved that neither comfortable cottages, ample provisions for comfortable living, nor yet coming here for weeks of relaxation from business and for the improvement of health, prevent the original objects of a camp-meeting from being attained, if we come here trusting in God, and if ministers and people enter into Christian labors as the fathers did, and as we should do.

Monday Morning. It was thought that more than thirty thousand different persons had visited for a longer or shorter time these grounds within the last two or three months. This morning was lovely. The closing service took place at eight o'clock. Prayer and remarks by the presiding officer; singing by the Hutchinsons. A collection of one hundred and sixty dollars was taken to aid in building a church in Minnesota. During the day it was made up to three hundred dollars. There was an old-fashioned marching around the circle, and leave-taking, hand-shaking, and singing. Many of us left, but some still remained, and meetings were announced for them, to be held during the day. But the camp-meeting proper was now closed.

During this camp-meeting excellent order had been maintained, as usual. Several of the State Police had been in attendance, having their headquarters in the camp. They were prompt in arresting the few violators of law, the overt acts of whom came to their knowledge, bringing them before a trial justice, who as promptly, evidence being given, dealt out even-handed justice to the offenders.

Some time previous to the commencement of the camp-meeting this year, the contract, — the negotiation of which was begun last year, — for lands, wood and cleared, north-westerly from the camp ground, was matured. Some fifty-five acres were thus purchased, not by the Association, but by persons connected with the meeting, the transaction being designed to be in the interest of the Association and of the camp-meeting. Subsequently, the number of the Company, which was named the "Vineyard Grove Company," was very considerably increased, others taking shares, and other purchases were made; so that the company now owned two hundred acres or more. They have proceeded to lay out their grounds into lots, parks, and avenues, reserving a large area in a well-wooded part, to be cleared and fitted for preaching services whenever needed. Probably there will always be preaching there as well as at the central stand on the great days of the meeting. Twelve thousand dollars' worth of lots have already been sold, and men are at work clearing up the grounds. This section is more elevated than any of the neighboring lands, and is to be known hereafter as " *The Vineyard High Lands.*"

The company have fixed the amount of their capital stock at twelve thousand dollars. They have voted to give one tenth part of all the proceeds of sales for the first year to the " Preachers' Aid Society" of the Providence Conference. Members of the Company design the enterprise for the benefit of the camp-meeting; and it is not impossible that, when the entire arrangements are mature, it will be formally annexed to the encampment grounds. The Company design petitioning the Massachusetts Legislature for the right to extend a wharf from their premises to the depth of eighteen feet of water — sufficient to admit to it the large steamers passing through the Sound from New York to Portland. They have already commenced making the preliminary arrangements for constructing it. They design also to build a bridge, when needed, across the pond, and a plank walk or road from the head of their wharf to the existing camp ground. The entire grounds of this Company are to be under the same rules as those of the Camp-meeting Association.

It is in contemplation to erect a large building near the wharf. The Company design petitioning for an act of incorporation, the corporate name to be "The Vineyard Grove Corporation." Several gentlemen of wealth, and some clergymen, are members of the Company. The entire list of members is as follows: L. Whitney, Jr., of Watertown; George F. Gavitt, of North Dighton; John D. Flint and J. D. King, of Fall River; William H. Phillips, L. T. Talbot, L. B. Bates, and J. Burt, of Taunton; Henry Baylies, of Providence, R. I.; Sirson P. Coffin, Richard L. Pease, and Rufus H. Davis, of Edgartown; F. P. Pond, F. Homer, Noah Tripp, and Caleb L. Ellis, of New Bedford; N. Wales, of Stoughton; C. Washburn, of East Weymouth; J. French, J. Q. Maynard, and D. E. Smith, M. D., of Brooklyn, N. Y.; Samuel C. Brown, of Warren, R. I.; and C. H. Sumner, of Boston.

The Oak Bluffs Company are enjoying great prosperity in the sale of cottage lots, having sold some three hundred. It is in contemplation by them to put up, near their wharf, a large hotel.

Propositions have been made to parties owning lands on both sides of the encampment for the purchase of *acres*, rather than mere cottage lots, for the purpose of having establishments on a larger scale. At the same time the camp ground proper is filling up to repletion, and must, we think, should no accident befall it, always remain the *nucleus* of this great summer resort, although some think the "High Lands" will take the lead.

It is matter for gratitude that, while this great modern Bethesda is, in its surroundings, becoming so extensively populated, those who come here are of the best classes of society. So it is at Oak Bluffs, and the Vineyard Grove, as well as on the Association's grounds. Some one, near the close of the late camp-meeting, expressing admiration at the excellent order maintained here, was replied to by another, that the people who come hither are good citizens at home; it was not strange, therefore, that they should be such here.

About three hundred acres are now owned by the different parties, the purchase of which has grown out of this camp-meeting interest. The place is, indeed, unique; the progress has been wonderful; and the gatherings here, consisting, as they do, of people and clergymen from different parts of the country, are quite "national."

There is no reason why those wishing a good summer resort should not come to this locality, but there are many reasons (some of which are elsewhere given) why they should. And if many of the irreligious come, there is the greater opportunity for Christian labor; and both the ministry and the laity sojourning here, and those attending the camp-meeting, of whatever religious name, should, instead of being intimidated by the numbers, seize upon it as a golden privilege of doing a great work for the Master, and for the salvation of their fellow-beings. May the associations here formed be happily consummated in the world of light and blessedness above.

BY-LAWS

Of the Martha's Vineyard Camp-Meeting Association, as amended August, 1869.

ARTICLE 1. The associates named in the first section of the act of incorporation of the Martha's Vineyard Camp-Meeting Association shall be, the pastor in charge for the time being of each Methodist Episcopal Society represented on the camp-ground by a society tent, or tent's company, the Presiding Elders of the Providence, Sandwich, and New Bedford Districts, and one lay member of each of said societies, who shall be chosen annually by the Quarterly Conference, or the Stewards' or Leaders' Meeting, and the Board of Directors, Treasurer, and Agent.

ART. 2. Said Association shall hold an annual meeting at such time and place as shall be decided upon by the President and Board of Directors, at which meeting they shall elect, by ballot, a President, Clerk, and Treasurer. The Clerk shall be sworn to a faithful discharge of his duties. At the first meeting of the Association, after the adoption of these articles, they shall elect, by ballot, a Board of Directors, consisting of eighteen, all of whom shall be members in good standing of the Methodist Episcopal Church, residing within the limits of the Providence, New Bedford, and Sandwich Districts, one third of whom shall be ministers in the regular work, and two thirds of whom shall be laymen.

One third of the said Board of Directors, ministers and laymen, shall hold their office for three years, one third for two years, and one third for one year; and annually, thereafter, the Association shall elect by ballot six Directors, two ministers and four laymen, for the term of three years.

ART. 3. The time for holding the annual camp-meeting shall be fixed by the Presiding Elders of the Providence and New Bedford Districts and the Chairman of the Board of Directors; and during the continuance of the said meeting the President of this Association shall have the sole charge and direction of the religious meetings.

The said Board of Directors shall, annually, at their first meeting after the annual meeting of the Association, organize by the election of Chairman and Clerk. They shall, also, at such time as they may think proper, annually elect by ballot an Agent of the Association, prescribe the duties of his office, and fix his compensation.

The said Board of Directors shall have the control and direction of all the financial matters connected with the Association, and shall have the sole charge of police regulations, and see that the laws made for the protection of camp-meetings are duly enforced.

They shall have authority to issue leases, or cause the same to be issued, for the erection of tents and buildings upon the grounds of the Association, upon such terms and conditions as to them may seem proper, and to make such assessments upon the said tents and buildings as may from time to time be necessary to defray the expenses of the corporation, and they shall at each annual meeting of the Association make a full and complete report of all their doings.

Vacancies in the Board, occasioned by death, resignation, or otherwise, may be filled by the remaining members; but such election to fill a vacancy shall not extend beyond the next annual meeting of the Association.

Seven members shall constitute a quorum at any meeting for the transaction of business.

ART. 4. The Board of Directors shall annually appoint the following, together with such other committees as may be necessary: 1. A committee on lots, who shall have charge of the laying out of tent and cottage lots; 2. A police committee, whose duty it shall be to have charge of the police arrangements, see that they are proper and sufficient at all times, and appoint such day and night watch as may be necessary for the peace and security of person and property; 3. A fire committee, whose duty it shall be to inspect all buildings upon the ground, to see that proper precaution is taken to guard against fire, and to devise such measures as may be practicable for the extinguishment of fire, should any occur; 4. A sanitary committee, who shall prescribe such rules and regulations as may be necessary to secure the health and comfort of all residents upon the ground; 5. A transportation committee, whose duty it shall be to make all necessary arrangements with railroads and steamboats for the transportation of persons and property; 6. An auditing committee, who shall annually examine the books and accounts of the Agent and Treasurer, and report thereon to the Board of Directors. All of which committees shall be under the direction of the Board of Directors.

ART. 5. The Clerk of the Association shall make a full and complete record of all business transactions at the meetings of the Association.

The Clerk of the Board of Directors shall keep a separate record of all business transactions by the Board, which records, both of the Association and Directors, shall be open for the inspection of members of the Association at any time.

The Treasurer shall hold all moneys belonging to the Association, paying out none except upon the order of the Board of Directors; and he shall make to the Association an annual report of the transactions for the year, which report shall be recorded by the Clerk of the Association.

The Board of Directors shall give in their annual report a clear and concise statement of the condition of the corporation at the time of making such report.

ART. 6. A special meeting of the Association shall be called by the President on the written request of five members of the Board of Directors.

ART. 7. These By-Laws may be altered or amended at any meeting of the Association by a vote of two thirds of the members present and voting thereon, notice of the same having been given at a previous meeting.

OFFICERS OF THE ASSOCIATION,

Elected August 24, 1869.

Rev. Samuel C. Brown, *President.*
George L. Westgate, *Clerk.*
Jeremiah Pease, *Treasurer.*
Geo. F. Gavitt, *Chairman of Board of Directors.*

DIRECTORS AS THEY NOW STAND.

For Three Years.
Rev. Fred'k Upham,
Rev. Louis B. Bates,
John D. Flint,
Wm. A. Wardwell,
Jacob Burt,
Jeremiah Pease.

For Two Years.
Rev. S. C. Brown,
Rev. J. D. King,
George F. Gavitt,
William B. Lawton,
Noah Tripp,
Pardon M. Stone.

For One Year.
Rev. C. H. Titus,
Rev. E. S. Stanley,
John Kendrick,
James Davis,
R. C. Brown,
C. L. Ellis.

CAMP-MEETING RULES.

1. Applications for license to erect a building or tent, from persons not members of the Association, must be accompanied by a written recommendation signed by three official members of the Methodist Episcopal Church nearest the place of residence of the applicant, or three members of the Association.

2. The ground within the circle of tents is sacredly set apart for religious worship; and during public service at the stand, all walking to and fro, or gathering together for conversation, is strictly prohibited.

3. At the ringing of the bell for public service, all loud conversation or other exercises in the tents and cottages must cease.

4. The hours for preaching shall be ten o'clock A. M., and two and seven P. M.

5. There snall be family devotions in each society tent morning and evening, with the reading of the Scriptures; and occupants of cottages and private tents are requested to attend regularly upon the same.

6. The bell will ring each morning at half past five o'clock for rising, and each evening at ten o'clock for retiring, when all vocal exercises must cease, and all persons not having lodgings within the encampment must immediately retire from the ground.

7. There shall be no smoking of tobacco in the society tents, or within the circle of said tents.

8. A light shall be kept burning at each cottage

and tent all night, whenever said cottage or tent is occupied.

9. The occupants of each cottage and tent, before retiring at night, shall cause a bucket of water to be placed outside of the same, near the front entrance, during the entire occupancy of the said cottage or tent, for use in case of fire.

10. There shall be a superintendent appointed by each tent's company, whose duty it shall be to preserve order in his tent, in accordance with the regulations of the meeting.

RESOLVES

Passed by the Association, August 23, 1869.

Resolved, That the Agent notify all owners of cottages and tents that they will be held responsible for the conduct of any persons to whom the cottage or tent is let, and any violation of the rules of the meeting or conditions of the lease by the persons occupying shall work a forfeiture of the lease. If any conduct unbecoming the place or its objects shall be allowed in said cottage or tent, it shall be immediately vacated and closed.

Also, that the owner of any cottage or tent, wishing to let it, be requested to let the Association have the first offer of the same; and the owner letting a cottage or tent shall give to the Agent the name and residence of the person to whom it is let.

www.ingramcontent.com/pod-product-compliance
Lightning Source LLC
Chambersburg PA
CBHW022355040426
42450CB00005B/186